POLITICS OF DECONSTRUCTION

POLITICS OF DECONSTRUCTION

A New Introduction to Jacques Derrida

Susanne Lüdemann

Translated by Erik Butler

STANFORD UNIVERSITY PRESS

STANFORD, CALIFORNIA

Stanford University Press
Stanford, California

English translation © 2014 by the Board of Trustees of the Leland Stanford
Junior University. All rights reserved.

Politics of Deconstruction was originally published in German in 2011 under the
title *Jacques Derrida zur Einführung* © 2011, Junius Verlag, Hamburg.

Printed in the United States of America on acid-free, archival-quality paper

Library of Congress Cataloging-in-Publication Data

Lüdemann, Susanne, 1960– author.
[Jacques Derrida zur Einführung. English]
    Politics of deconstruction : a new introduction to Jacques Derrida / Susanne
Lüdemann ; translated by Erik Butler.
        pages cm
    "Originally published in German in 2011 under the title *Jacques Derrida zur
Einführung.*"
    Includes bibliographical references.
    ISBN 978-0-8047-8412-2 (cloth : alk. paper)
    ISBN 978-0-8047-8413-9 (pbk. : alk. paper)
    1. Derrida, Jacques. 2. Deconstruction. 3. Criticism. I. Title.
B2430.D484L83613 2014
194—dc23
                                                                    2014008594

ISBN 978-0-8047-9302-5 (electronic)

I dedicate the American edition of this book to my former colleagues and students at the University of Chicago, where most of it was written, and especially to those who participated in my graduate class on Derrida in winter 2011.

Contents

Preface: Derrida's Legacy

> It is one thing to determine and describe the opinions of philosophers. It is an entirely different thing to talk through [*durchsprechen*] with them what they are saying, and that means, that of which they speak.
> —Martin Heidegger, "What is Philosophy?"
>
> We must begin *wherever we are*. . . . *Wherever we are*: in a text where we already believe ourselves to be.[1]

When he died in Paris in October 2004, the philosopher Jacques Derrida was a kind of media star. Auditors from all over the world flocked to his lectures and crowded the halls of the École Normale Supérieure, and later those of the École des Hautes Etudes en Sciences Sociales. When he spoke of matters such as the "politics of friendship" or "questions of responsibility," a battery of devices recorded his every word. Derrida, whose writings have been translated into forty languages, held guest-professorships and lectured across the globe, received honorary degrees from twenty-five universities, and gave countless interviews on philosophy and current events. Two films were made about him, which presented the avid public with a portrait of both the thinker and the man himself, in private life.

For a philosopher—even one as prolific as Derrida—such publicity is unusual. The time has passed when philosophy played a leading role in the public sphere. Today, a lot of people are more likely to seek answers to the "big questions" from biology or the neurosciences. Moreover, Derrida's celebrity stands in inverse relation to the difficulty his texts present. While "deconstruction" became a fashionable label for theoretical works in the 1980s and 1990s, few people actually bothered reading the texts that received this appellation. Indeed, the attention the media paid to the reception of Derrida's writings often proved a hindrance inasmuch as they gave rise, especially in Germany and the United States, to dismissals of the philosopher as a charlatan and of his concerns as so many rhetorical obfuscations; needless to say, discounting Derrida in this way spared his critics the effort of actually reading what he had written.

The book at hand is *not* meant as a substitute for reading Derrida's texts. Such an intention would be misplaced for at least two reasons: to begin with, the body of texts that appeared under the name of "Jacques Derrida" is too vast to be discussed and commentated—much less summed up—in an introductory work. It includes, depending how one reckons, between twenty-five and forty books, several collections of essays, and countless lectures and articles; and that calculation leaves aside the thousands of pages of unpublished material housed at the Critical Theory Archive of the University of California at Irvine. Moreover, the subject itself makes a synoptic account impossible. Once one has taken to heart the lesson of *reading* that deconstruction offers—a lesson that constitutes the project above all else—one cannot consider a commentary to provide an adequate substitute, no matter how knowledgeable, learned, and consecrated by academic authority it may be. After Derrida, one should not presume to reformulate what an author has already said (or intended to say) in a more concise, systematic, or clear manner; attempting to do so can only occur at the price of misrecognizing and betraying the object of commentary (cf. below, 2.3).

Accordingly, this slim volume is not meant to replace other introductory works, which have their own merits and rights. Instead, it seeks to provide the reader with a means of finding his or her own way into Derrida's work—by retracing the points of entry that the author herself has found over the years. These modes of approach are *ways among others*—paths of one particular reading marked by the contingencies of academic and personal history. If it is true that reading means finding "a signifying structure that critical reading should *produce*"[2] in the first place (see below, 2.2), then no other way of proceeding even exists. Of course, the book was not written without consideration of those for whom it is intended. Above all, it is addressed to students of the humanities, as well as parties within and outside the academy interested in philosophy and politics, who desire "guidance"—explanations of concepts, preconditions, and historical and thematic contexts that are not self-evident. This study seeks to strike a balance between determining and describing "opinions," on the one hand, and "talking them through," on the other.

In keeping with Derrida's insights, such discussion involves "writing-" or "working through" in the Freudian sense—a mode of inheritance that entails appropriating and passing along what has been handed down. Despite his reputation as a "nihilist" and a "destroyer of tradition," Derrida repeatedly emphasized that we are the heirs of a philosophical and political tradition for which we must assume responsibility. However, he also stressed that the legacy cannot simply be taken as a self-evident matter; it is inherently heterogeneous, contradictory, and divided. "An inheritance is never gathered together," one reads in *Specters of Marx* (1994),

it is never one with itself. Its presumed unity, if there is one, can consist only in the *injunction to reaffirm by choosing.* "One must" means one must filter, sift, criticize, one must sort out several different possibles that inhabit the same injunction. [. . .] *If the readability of a legacy were given, natural, transparent, univocal, if it did not call for and at the same time defy interpretation, we would never have anything to inherit from it.* We would be affected by it as by a cause—natural or genetic. One always inherits from a secret—which says "read me, will you ever be able to do so?"[3]

The same holds for Derrida's legacy—an immense corpus of texts that do not yield the unity of a book (or the book-as-an-integrated-whole, an *oeuvre*). Derrida's writings expound, vary, and abandon themes, which are then taken up in other books and lectures, where they are treated again, further modified, and considered in a new light. In this way, a footnote provides the point of departure for another text, a preface points to a book yet to be written. Such experimentation with textual forms "possesses" a "method" only insofar as it actively negates the classical conception of philosophy as a series of deductive steps leading to the recognition and demonstration of the truth (for reasons that will be discussed).

Derrida's work does not yield a system of theses that one might reconstruct in keeping with the logic of a development from point A to point B. Rather, it resembles an open network of references and correspondences—a "fabric of traces"[4] in a space of writing and thinking where readings overlap, motifs echo each other, and lines of interpretation intersect, change direction, and then diverge. In a certain sense, this space of writing and thinking occupies the space of the tradition whose inheritor Derrida understood himself to be, into which he inscribed his own works—above all, by a process of reading. For Derrida, *reading* (*reading* as *inheriting,* and *inheriting* as transformative transmission) represents philosophical praxis *tout court.* For this reason, the book at hand considers it essential to explain what *reading,* in the deconstructive sense of the word, means. It lies in the nature of the matter (insofar as the author of this book follows the deconstructive project) that this can only occur *by reading,* and this is why the following offers more exemplary readings of texts than attempts to summarize them (i.e., write about or "describe" "opinions").

At the same time, the study represents a compromise with classical, propaedeutic form inasmuch as it respects chronology. After an introductory chapter on the philosophical-historical preconditions of deconstruction, the readings follow, for the most part, the sequence in which Derrida's texts were written or published. Proceeding in this fashion makes it possible to discern a certain succession of themes and a shift in focus. Derrida's writings up to the 1980s are devoted above all to the concepts of the sign, writing, text, and difference, which are *displaced* in order to deconstruct the metaphysics of presence. The texts of the late 1980s until Derrida's death, on the other hand, more frequently address ethical and political topics, which are explored in conjunction with the undeconstructible premises of deconstruction (cf. Third Approach). How and why the critique of language is inseparable from ethics—how and why the deconstruction of ontology connects with the project of thinking a "democracy to come"—will also be our concern.

A word about what is *not* treated on the following pages is in order. Among Derrida's "main" works, this includes *Glas* (1974), his engagement with Hegel and Jean Genet, and two books that contribute to (the critique of) aesthetics and the philosophy of the body: *Truth in Painting* (1978) and *On Touching—Jean-Luc Nancy* (2000). Likewise, Derrida's discussion of Husserl, the focus of his first publications, is treated only in passing. Finally, the matter of deconstruction and psychoanalysis would have deserved a chapter of its own, as would the topic of deconstruction and literature (even though attention is paid to the significance of both for situating deconstruction in the contemporary theoretical landscape). The omissions stem from limitations of space, as well as from personal decisions that deem some matters more directly relevant than others. Among the different possibilities inhering in Derrida's injunction, I have given preference to those that seem more likely than others to have an effect extending beyond the borders of the academy—those that entail changes in our ways of thinking and acting. In this, I follow Derrida's own articulation of the role of deconstruction, which

> would like, in order to be consistent with itself, not to remain enclosed in purely speculative, theoretical, academic discourses but rather . . . to aspire to something more consequential, to *change* things and to intervene in an efficient and responsible, though always, of course, very mediated way, not only in the profession but in what one calls the *cité*, the *polis*, and more generally the world.[5]

Whether this, after the author's death, will prove possible, depends most of all on the readiness of those who have survived Derrida to *inherit* from him, read his writings, work through them, critique them, and reaffirm his legacy *by choosing*.

Even if such a decision, in the final instance, must be undertaken independently, an introduction may still help one to find "one's own way." The undertaking is not easy, especially from my own, German, perspective. In Germany, the university system never paid much heed to structuralism, poststructuralism, or psychoanalysis. In Germany as well as in the US, linguists read everyone but Saussure, psychologists read everyone but Freud, and academic philosophers have never been able to make much of Derrida (among other reasons, because of omissions practiced by their colleagues in the aforementioned fields). Not much has changed since I was a student in the 1980s—the buzz in the media surrounding Derrida as a public intellectual, now as then, amounts to deafness and resistance to the matters that concerned him.

It reflects my own interpretation when I describe the reasons underlying deconstruction as the attempt to find a responsible form of philosophizing "after Auschwitz," to paraphrase Theodor W. Adorno. Derrida does not explicitly voice this intention anywhere in his work (except, perhaps, somewhere in his unedited papers), and he never mentioned Adorno more than in passing (and that, according to reliable sources, mainly in the late, still-unpublished seminars). The differences between Adorno and Derrida are, of course, significant. In a word, Adorno views the "nonidentical" as an unredeemed or unreconciled form of identity; for Derrida—who refers to it by the name of *différance*—it represents a form of auto-affection that, while irreducible, must be affirmed. All the same, it is no accident that a form of connectivity exists between Critical Theory and deconstruction, for both projects seek to explore the consequences of twentieth-century (European) catastrophe. That is, both projects seek *to assume this inheritance—especially this inheritance—in view of a future in which nothing of the like should occur again.*

We are not free to reject this responsibility. Indeed, as Derrida says, we are responsible to past and future alike, whether we wish to be and whether we know it, or not. It is this condition of obligation that makes it necessary to read. And so, wherever we are, we must begin there. Somewhere, wherever we are: in a text where we already believe ourselves to be—for example, in this one, here.

POLITICS OF DECONSTRUCTION

First Approach: Generations, Genealogies, Translations, and Contexts

> I believe that this difficulty with belonging, one would almost say of identification, affects the whole of Jacques Derrida's oeuvre, and it seems to me that 'the deconstruction of the proper' is the very thought of this, its thinking affection.[1]

1.1 From the "Three-H Generation" to the "Three Masters of Suspicion"

Jacques Derrida was born July 15, 1930, in El-Biar, near Algiers. His parents were assimilated Sephardic Jews, which inscribed the question of belonging into his life in multiple ways. Having grown up French among Arabs, and Jewish among Maghreb Muslims, Derrida first arrived in Paris at the age of twenty-two, shortly before the Algerian War of Independence; as a French Algerian (or *pied-noir*—"blackfoot" in colloquial parlance), he did not belong to the establishment there, either. Even when he had achieved worldwide fame, Derrida's position in the French university system remained relatively modest, although ultimately this was due more to his controversial philosophical theses than to his origins. Before relocating to Paris, Derrida—who did not know Hebrew and never attended a yeshiva—experienced his connection to Judaism primarily through anti-Semitic ascriptions from without. Under the Vichy regime, Algerian Jews had lost their French citizenship, and Jewish children had been turned away from schools (as one principal explained: "French culture is not made for little Jews"[2]). Perhaps it is not unwarranted to see in these biographical facts an important motor of Derrida's thought, which can be designated—in an initial, summary fashion—as a *thinking of difference* in all its forms.

Derrida came to Paris in 1952 as a student at the École Normale Supérieure, where he also taught from 1965 until 1984. The Parisian philosophical landscape was shaped by the so-called "Three-H Generation"— that is, French disciples and interpreters of Hegel, Husserl, and Heidegger. At the time, the dominant orientations in philosophy were existentialism (Jean-Paul Sartre, Simone de Beauvoir, Albert Camus), French phenomenology (Maurice Merleau-Ponty, Emmanuel Levinas, Paul Ricoeur), and structuralism (Claude Lévi-Strauss's structural anthropology and Jacques Lacan's structural psychoanalysis). Politically, engagement with the Algerian War and Stalinist Communism set the tone of the day. Subsequently, especially in the 1960s, a transition occurred from the "Three-H Generation" to the "three masters of suspicion": Marx, Nietzsche, and Freud. This shift is associated with the emergence of what has come to be known as poststructuralism, a grouping that includes—besides Michel Foucault, Gilles Deleuze, Jean Baudrillard, Jean-François Lyotard, and others— Jacques Derrida himself. (To be sure, such classifications are not easy: one may rightfully hesitate to call Ricoeur a phenomenologist, and Lacan is every bit as much a "poststructuralist" as he is a "structuralist"—or maybe neither. Roland Barthes, who is counted among poststructuralists in standard reference works, understood himself as a structuralist. Many teachers and fellow travelers of Derrida and his contemporaries—for example, Maurice Blanchot—defy such categorizations altogether.)

It is remarkable that the "triumvirates" French philosophy uses to count its generations consist exclusively of German-language thinkers. However, this in no way means that French philosophy of the twentieth century lacks originality and independence. Rather, it is in France that the most important consequences of the grand philosophical projects of modernity—from Hegel's *Phenomenology of Spirit* to Nietzsche's "transvaluation of all values," Heidegger's fundamental ontology, and Freud's metapsychology—have been drawn. After the Second World War, French philosophers took up radical ways of thinking about modernity that began in Germany and were interrupted—to lasting effect—by National Socialism, and they followed them through to their "postmodern" consequences.

Post-war German philosophy, on the other hand, produced Frankfurt School Critical Theory, which drew chiefly on Hegel and Marx, until, in the mid-1980s, readings of Nietzsche, Heidegger, and Freud from France introduced changes to the intellectual horizon.

It is significant, for the productive appropriation of the German "triumvirate" that occurred in France, that the most important texts often were not readily accessible. In some cases, they had only recently been translated (the first French edition of *Phenomenology of Spirit* appeared in 1947; the first complete translation of *Being and Time* did not come out until the 1980s). In other cases, key works had not been published at all—for example, many writings by Husserl. Instead of having complete editions laden with the interpretations of academic authorities, French readers dealt with a quarry of fragments, partial translations, manuscripts, and works in the German original; inevitably, differences of culture and language were inscribed in the fabric of every translation.

Derrida's path through this multi-faceted intellectual and political landscape did not follow a straight line. His first years in Paris were also shaped by profound personal crises. The only constant, from the beginning, was a rejection of Sartre's existentialism, from which Heidegger had also distanced himself in the *Letter on Humanism* (addressed to the French philosopher and Germanist Jean Beaufret in 1946). The *Letter* marks a decisive date for the intellectual debate in France, because it not only includes a self-interpretation (Heidegger's account of his so-called *turn [Kehre]* in the 1930s), but also, immediately "after Auschwitz," initiated the discussion on humanism. Beaufret had asked Heidegger whether, after what had happened, it was still possible to find a new sense for the term. Heidegger responded by roundly critiquing humanism as an essentially metaphysical enterprise that, because of its built-in limitations, missed the "essence" of human existence. His reply was also directed against Sartre, who, in a polemical piece from the previous year—*Is Existentialism a Humanism?*—had unequivocally answered his own question in the affirmative. This debate stands at the origin of much talk—which has been as popular as it has been mistaken—about the "end of man" and the "death of the subject" (most often attributed to Foucault). In Germany, the discourse has contributed to characterizations of French poststructuralism not only as anti-humanist but as anti-human (i.e., as irrationalist and hostile to Enlightenment).

Among other things, this introduction means to combat such sim-
plifications—at least as far as Derrida is concerned. For the most part,
they result from imprecise readings (when they are not a pretext to avoid
the work of reading altogether). In a lecture entitled "Finis Hominis"—
delivered in April 1968, against the background of Parisian student riots,
failed peace negotiations in Vietnam, and the assassination of Martin
Luther King, Jr.—Derrida brought philosophy and politics together when
he took up the humanism debate and distanced himself from both Sartre
and Heidegger. This talk also renders idle another allegation often leveled
against Derrida—that deconstruction is "aestheticizing" and therefore
apolitical. As we will see later on, nothing could be more mistaken.

Derrida's first writings were devoted to Heidegger's teacher, Edmund
Husserl. In his 1954 dissertation, *The Problem of Genesis in Husserl's Philosophy*, Derrida translated Appendix III of Husserl's late work, *The Crisis of
the European Sciences and Transcendental Phenomenology,* and provided an
introduction considerably longer than the primary text.[3] In 1967, Derrida
published *Speech and Phenomena: An Essay on the Problem of the Sign in
Husserl's Philosophy*. This work articulates the critique of phonocentrism,
logocentrism, and presence to which *Of Grammatology* (which appeared
the same year and remains Derrida's best-known book) opposes a "science
of writing." Two essays on Husserl from the same time warrant mention
as well: "'Genesis and Structure' and Phenomenology" and "Form and
Meaning: A Note on the Phenomenology of Language."

However, this introductory chapter concerns not Husserl, but Heidegger, Nietzsche, and Freud, whose projects Derrida inherited in *methodological* terms. (Later, Derrida turned away from Husserl altogether; of
phenomenological authors, only Emmanuel Levinas remained important
to him.[4]) In addition, structuralism and the "linguistic turn" provide
immediate preconditions for his poststructuralist critique of the sign. The
selection is not arbitrary. While incomplete, it permits us, in brief traits, to
sketch the intellectual horizons of deconstruction, both as a *philosophical
project* and as a *practice of reading*. Against this background, a paradigm
shift occurred in the second half of the nineteenth- and the first half of the
twentieth centuries. Stated summarily, it may be characterized as a change
from thinking in terms of identity to thinking along lines of difference,
a move from thinking about sameness to thinking in terms of the other,

and reorientation away from the primacy of consciousness toward the primacy of language. The shift occurred as a radical self-critique within the philosophical tradition. Its most conspicuous symptom is a somewhat apocalyptic tone—the end of art and history (Hegel), the end of philosophy (Heidegger), the end of man (Nietzsche, Heidegger), the death of God (Nietzsche), the death of the subject (Foucault), and the death of the author (Barthes). The break is evident when one compares Hegel, the last systematic philosopher (for whom the end of history was synonymous with its fulfillment), and Nietzsche, the first diagnostician of the "rise of nihilism."

Ever since Nietzsche, the philosophical tradition that began with Plato and Aristotle has no longer been understood as a historical progression leading to a final system of knowledge and insight, but as a problematic inheritance whose ontological and epistemological value stands to be questioned. In the years surrounding 1900, representative words of debate are the "transvaluation of all values" (Nietzsche), "crisis of the spirit" (Valéry), linguistic crisis, "crisis of the European sciences" (Husserl), and "decline of the West" (Spengler). The reasons for the heightened sense of collapse are too numerous to be discussed here. Political events, wars (above all, the First World War), economic disaster, and the development of modern mass society play as a great a role as what Max Weber (among others) diagnosed as the increasing rationalization and "disenchantment" of the world. In what follows, we must limit ourselves to the self-critique of philosophical thinking relevant to Derrida.

1.2 The "Destruction of the History of Ontology" and Dasein as "In-Between" (Heidegger)

Derrida first used the term "deconstruction" in the book that made him famous: *Of Grammatology*. Although he observes that the word already existed in the French language, it was rarely used. Derrida employed it to translate two other concepts: first, Heidegger's program calling for the "destruction" of the history of ontology, and, second, Freud's concept of "dissociation." Thereby, he invoked two very different predecessors, whose very different concepts his project simultaneously combines and interprets. We shall begin with the first.

In *Being and Time* (1926), Heidegger had declared the "task" of undertaking the "destruction of the history of ontology." Since Aristotle, Heidegger wrote, ontology—a term comprised of two Greek words: *on* ("being," the present participle of *einai* ["to be"]) and *logos* ("reasoning," "word," "speech")—has been understood to concern *beings* alone. Therefore, he argues, philosophical tradition has missed—and obscured—the question of the sense of Being itself. For Aristotle, ontology represents "first philosophy" (*prote philosophia*) or "theological science" (*episteme theologike*). Elsewhere, Aristotle calls ontology "general metaphysics," which he defines as follows:

There is a kind of science whose remit is being *qua* being and the things pertaining to that which is *per se*. This science is not the same as any of the departmental disciplines. For none of these latter engages in this *general* speculation about that which is *qua* that which is. Rather, they delimit some section of what is and study its accidental features (a prime example is mathematics). We, however, are investigating principles and fundamental causes, and these must evidently pertain *per se* to a kind of nature.[5]

Thus, ontology or metaphysics represents the most general of intellectual disciplines. It does not investigate a specific realm of Being (as, for example, biology and physics do—or, more recently, psychology and sociology); instead, it explores the attributes characterizing all that exists, insofar as it exists. For Aristotle, these attributes include "substance," "quantity," "quality," "relation," "where," "when," "having," "doing," and "being-affected" (the so-called "categories," or, in Latin, "predicates"). However, Being itself does not represent a category, since the concept of mere existence counts as *empty*. For Aristotle and the entire tradition that follows after him, the concept of Being adds nothing. Whatever we imagine, we picture as already existing. In this way, Being is implicit in beings, but it cannot be separated from them nor can it stand on its own. Linguistic usage reflects that it only represents the copula ("link") of judgment—something connecting the subject of a sentence and its predicate. If I say, "The sky is blue," "Socrates is a human being," or "Deconstruction is a philosophical method," all these sentences have the form: A (subject) *is* B (predicate). The existence of the subjects ("sky," "Socrates," "deconstruction") is expressed—it lies in the tiny word "is"—but only has the function of tying together A and B. An utterance of the type "A is" ("The sky is," "Socrates is") would, in a standard, ontological conception, be either meaningless or superfluous, since it expresses nothing that is not already contained in A. In this view, referring to something and referring to it as something in existence mean the same thing, even if what is being referred to no longer exists (like Socrates, who has died) or does not, in fact, exist yet (like the sky tomorrow): past and future are modalities of Being conceived in terms of the present.

Here, Heidegger stresses that the "sense of Being" should by no means count as something as self-evident as metaphysical tradition claims. His philosophy does not address beings as beings, but focuses instead on what "is"—the unthought basis of Being that the occidental tradition does not explore, yet which determines our understanding of beings. Heidegger calls his project in *Being and Time* "fundamental ontology"; it represents the attempt to get behind ontology as the supposed first philosophy and to uncover its preconditions. This uncovering requires "destruction"—not wholesale annihilation, but rather, following the Latin verb *destruere*, the act of undoing or taking-apart—the patient removal of layers of philosophical inheritance, back to pre-Socratic fundamentals:

If the question of Being is to have its own history made transparent, then this hardened tradition must be loosened up, and the concealments which it has brought about must be dissolved. We understand this task as one in which *by taking the question of Being as our clue* we are to destroy the traditional content of ancient ontology until we arrive at those primordial experiences in which we achieved our first ways of determining the nature of Being—the ways which have guided us ever since.

In thus demonstrating the origin of our basic ontological concepts by an investigation in which their "birth certificate" is displayed, we have nothing to do with a vicious relativizing of ontological standpoints. But this destruction is just as far from having the *negative* sense of shaking off the ontological tradition. We must, on the contrary, stake out the *positive* possibilities of that tradition, and this means keeping it within its *limits*; and these in turn are given factically in the way the question is formulated at the time, and in the way the possible field for investigation is thus bounded off. On its negative side, this destruction does not relate itself toward the past; its criticism is aimed at "today" and at the prevalent way of treating the history of ontology. . . . But to bury the past in nullity [*Nichtigkeit*] is not the purpose of this destruction; its aim is *positive*; its negative function remains unexpressed and indirect.[6]

This de-struction brings to light the implicit pre-understanding of Being as *presence*, which privileges the here-and-now (in linguistic terms, the "present tense"). In keeping with this pre-understanding, philosophical tradition has always understood the Being of what exists in terms of availability and objectivity. All that is, is conceived as a mass of things that are, in substance, identical with themselves—entities that somehow are, were, or will be available in the world. The ways we think depend so deeply on such a pre-understanding that it never becomes apparent how a certain *interpretation* of Being already underlies them. It seems that what is, is waiting there for us—"automatically," as it were. The sky, a desk, deconstruction—they just are. They may be, respectively, blue, wood, and difficult to understand, but no reasonable doubt seems possible that they are already parts of our surroundings—and that we, too, are available (or, to employ Heidegger's terminology, "present-at-hand" [*vorhanden*]) as a kind of thing ourselves. Indeed, the philosophical tradition, up to Hegel, conceived of the human being—the subject—as a substance identical with itself. This substance thinks and is therefore not simply a thing among others; rather, it encounters objects (and other subjects) in the world. All the same, it is still conceived as a substance (*res cogitans*, as Descartes put it), which assures itself of its own presence in the world and that of its objects by thinking. Many names have been given to this "thing that thinks" in the course of history—"subject," "spirit," "consciousness," "soul," "ego," "self," "person"—but in ontological terms, it has always been conceived as something whose being, explicitly or implicitly, has retained the meaning of presence and availability.[7]

Heidegger's "destruction" of the traditional understanding of Being begins precisely here. Heidegger remarks that what exists in "subjectlike" fashion, when it understands itself as present-at-hand, fundamentally misses its own, intrinsic way of being. For this reason, he avoids concepts like "subject" and "ego" and uses the term *Dasein* (literally: *being there*) instead. Above all, Dasein is the kind of being that we are "each one of us," and therefore the Being of this being is "always mine" (*je meines*). It is not "always mine" in the sense of my being present-at-hand to me and others, however, but in such a way that the "for-the-sake-of-which" of my being is this being itself.

Whereas an animal, a tree, and other entities simply *are* and do not pose the question of what possibilities inhabit them (indeed, they are not even able to pose this question), Dasein is distinguished by the fact that it asks for the "sense of Being"—above all for the sense of its "own" being. According to Heidegger, such Being and meaning are never simply given; in essence, they are potentiality, openness, projection, and possibility. Therefore, Dasein can never be understood ontologically as an "instance or special case of some genus of entities that are present-at-hand."[8] If, nevertheless, Heidegger says that the "essence" of Dasein lies in "existence,"[9] what he means does not coincide with the traditional concept of existence as comprised of objects present-at-hand. Later, to avoid misunderstanding and to emphasize the differences between his own philosophy and French existentialism—Sartre's magnum opus, *Being and Nothingness*, had appeared in 1943—Heidegger wrote *Ek-sistenz* instead of *Existenz*. (Derrida's neographism *différance*, in lieu of *différence* [cf. Chapter 2], may have followed this precedent.) In the *Letter on Humanism* (1954), Heidegger cautiously referred Jean Beaufret to what he had written in *Being and Time*—"the 'essence' of Dasein lies in its existence"—and he put "essence" in quotes to signal its problematic status.[10]

The literal meaning of the word "existence," which comes from Latin, is "standing out" or "standing outside." The way Heidegger writes the term emphasizes the eccentric condition of Dasein—its indeterminacy and "thrownness" (*Geworfenheit*) into an unknown present and future. In contrast to an animal, Dasein can "win" or "lose"[11] itself because of the "innate" lack of direction in its Being. Dasein has, as its "ownmost possibility" (*eigenste Möglichkeit*),[12] an authentic relationship to Being, but it can also fall short of realizing this potential and lapse into the boundless falsehood that Heidegger calls "the They" (*das Man*) and "idle talk" (*Gerede*)—what "everybody says" in keeping with prevailing opinions and prejudices. Heidegger counts the whole of modern science as "idle talk" insofar as it remains stuck in the traditional conception of Being. Neither psychology nor biology nor anthropology has considered man, Dasein, in terms other than those of the passed-down categories of something that exists as present-at-hand—whether as the subject of acts of reason or feelings, as a thinking life form, or as the creature of God.[13] How, then, is Heidegger's analysis of Dasein different from what is offered by these sciences?

Heidegger does not see Dasein as determined by categories, but through what he terms *existentialia*. They include "being-in-the-world" (*in-der-Welt-sein*), "situatedness" (or "state/condition," *Befindlichkeit*), "understanding" (*Verstand*), "discourse" (or "speech," *Rede*), "fallenness" (*Verfallenheit*), "anxiety" (or "dread," *Angst*), and "care" (or "concern," *Sorge*). *Existentialia* are not attributes belonging to Dasein as matters present-at-hand. Rather, they are forms in which Dasein realizes itself. It is readily apparent that this list contains what classical subject-philosophy considers accidents (that, is non-essential properties). *Understanding* and *discourse* can, if need be, correspond to terms of the Aristotelian definition of human being as *zoon logon echon*—the life form that thinks and speaks. However, Heidegger assigns them a different meaning altogether, and *situatedness, fallenness, anxiety,* and *care* represent something markedly different from what the tradition preceding him proposed as essential qualities of human beings. Heidegger explicitly states that these concepts should not be understood in a colloquial sense; rather, he insists that the terminology derives strictly from the basic structure of Dasein. It cannot be denied that affect comes into play, which philosophical tradition has considered to be comprised of secondary phenomena—and chiefly disruptive ones, which restrict the capacity for insight and moral judgment. Heidegger, however—and in contrast to his predecessors—emphasizes the world-disclosing function of situatedness (or, as he puts it elsewhere, "being attuned" [*Gestimmtheit*]). Situatedness provides the basis for the ways Dasein refers to itself and the world, and it is impossible to abstract it from this material state of being. Likewise, understanding and discourse (as the articulation of understanding) are never value-free or neutral: they signify determinate understanding and definite discourse, which are bound up in the sum of Dasein's relations to the world of which it forms a part.

Moreover, Heidegger employs the *existentialia* to understand Dasein in terms of its temporality—that is, in terms of *historicity*. Dasein is

— "always already" thrown into a world that was there before it came into being; it is, as a matter of course, situated within the transmission of culture,

— "ahead of itself" in that it *understands* the world and seizes or rejects the possibilities it offers,

— "among" all that is within the world, that is, among the things and human beings that give it immediate points of orientation.

Heidegger sees the "being of Dasein," which he denominates "care" or "concern" (*Sorge*), in the unity of these three temporal dimensions, and he defines "care/concern," in his personal idiom, as "ahead-of-itself-already-being-in (a world) as Being-alongside (beings encountered within-the-world) (*Sich-vorweg-schon-sein-in [der Welt] als Sein-bei [innerweltlich] begegnendem Seienden*)."[14] In the mode of care or concern, Dasein is no longer primarily determined by presence. Rather, as the dimension of what is at hand, presence belongs to the dimension of *fallenness*, where Dasein becomes oblivious and goes missing among the things of the world. Dasein's ability to exist "authentically," on the other hand, is determined by the future, toward which Dasein projects itself, and from which it comes toward itself. Insofar as this future only ends in the moment of death, Dasein is *always* its own future; it is *always* still pending and, for this reason, *never* a "fulfilled" presence identical with itself.

"It is essential to the basic constitution of Dasein that it comprises continuous incompletedness (*eine ständige Unabgeschlossenheit*)."[15] This refers, on the one hand, to all that lives—whatever comes into being (is born) and ceases to be; yet in contrast to an animal or plant, Dasein *knows* about its futurity—and that means, above all, that it also knows about its mortality. As the "utmost not-yet," death is also something not present-at-hand; instead, it stands in the offing for Dasein, which finds its relation to death in the condition of anxiety (*Befindlichkeit der Angst*).[16] In anxiety (before imminent death), Dasein experiences that the impossibility of its own existence represents its utmost condition of being. For Heidegger, therefore, the essence of Dasein is determined by death; it is "being-unto-death":

In anticipation [of the possibility of death] Dasein can first make certain of its ownmost Being in its totality—a totality which is not to be outstripped. Therefore the evidential character which belongs to the immediate givenness of Experiences, of the "I," or of consciousness, must necessarily lag behind the certainty which anticipation includes.[17]

The question of the "sense of Being" also arises out of this "anticipation" of (literally, "running ahead into" [*vorlaufen in*]) the possibility of death, out of Dasein's encounter with the possibility of not-being. This encounter brings Dasein, which is seized by anxiety, back to the bare fact of its "ownmost, isolated thrownness."[18] Likewise, the dimensions of present and past are disclosed to Dasein only with reference to the future. Coming back to itself from running ahead into the possibility of death, Dasein becomes cognizant of the finite temporality that constitutes it. It discovers itself as already being—and always having been—in the world, as being kept in suspense between thrownness and projection, birth and death, past and future. "The 'between' which relates to birth and death already lies *in the Being* of Dasein. [. . .] Thrownness and that Being towards death in which one either flees it or anticipates it, form a unity; and in this unity birth and death are 'connected' in a manner characteristic of Dasein. As care, Dasein *is* the 'between.'"[19]

As such a "between," however, Dasein is incontrovertibly nonidentical; it differs from itself. A being of this kind never can coincide with itself in the experience of full self-presence and identity. Heidegger's "destruction" of the history of ontology leads beyond the conceptions of subject and consciousness in classical philosophy. This is where Derrida's thought connects with his predecessor's.

1.3 The De-centering of the Subject and the Critique of Moral Values (Freud, Nietzsche)

As we have noted, "deconstruction" *translates* not only Heidegger's "destruction," but also Freud's concept of "dissociation" (*Dissoziation*, from the Latin verb meaning "to separate/split"). Unlike "the unconscious" or "repression," this notion is not particularly prominent in Freud's work. It was coined by the French psychiatrist Pierre Janet (1859–1947), for whom it designated the (pathological) disintegration and fragmentation of consciousness. (Thus, Freud's term "dissociation" is already a translation, which Derrida translates back into French.) Freud employs the concept only in his *Studies on Hysteria* (1895). In his later writings, he prefers the terms "breaking-up of the ego (*Aufsplitterung des Ich*), "ego-split" (*Ichspaltung*), or "division of consciousness" (*Bewusstseinsspaltung*)—among other reasons, because he wishes to highlight differences between his own understanding of psychic processes and the ideas of French psychiatry. There is no need to go into the details of the history of the notion. What is important is that Derrida, under the rubric of dissociation, refers to Freud's model for the psychic apparatus; in so doing, he gestures toward psychoanalysis as another way to move beyond the conceptions of consciousness that underlie traditional philosophy. Psychoanalysis, although it does not belong to philosophical tradition, is no less significant to deconstruction than its philosophical inheritance, properly speaking.

For Freud, the "breaking-up" or "splitting" of the ego results from so-called defense-processes—repression (*Verdrängung*), disavowal (*Verleugnung*), negation (*Verneinung*), and foreclosure (*Verwerfung*)—through which the ego banishes ideas, thoughts, and wishes (especially those with a sexual or aggressive content) that are incompatible with its conscious self-image. Freud observes these mechanisms at work in the mentally ill, but he leaves no room for doubt that they are also a normal component of psychic life. Therefore, from a psychoanalytic perspective, the splitting (or disassociation) of the psyche into conscious and unconscious parts is not an illness to be eliminated through therapy; rather, it is constitutive for the genesis of the subject, which *must* repress certain drives and desires (for Freud, these are, above all, the Oedipal wishes of childhood) in order to meet the demands of culture and reality. The neurotic, then, is not necessarily someone who represses "more" than others, but someone who represses particularly "badly": unmastered conflicts originating in the neurotic's childhood assume the form of psychic and somatic symptoms in adult life. Freud observes that the "offshoots of the unconscious" also find expression in the verbal slips and dreams of "normal" people. In this model of the psyche as a site of conflict, the ego is only one of several instances. Freud characterizes it as a "poor creature owing service to three masters and consequently menaced by three dangers: from the external world, from the libido of the id, and from the severity of the super-ego."[20] As a "frontier-creature" between three sources of danger, the ego occupies a space "in-between"—the "actual seat of anxiety."[21] It "represents what can be called prudence and reason" and is to a great extent conscious (if not entirely so); at the same time, however, the ego forms only a small part of otherwise unknown and unconscious psychic life, "more or less as the germinal disc rests upon the ovum,"[22] without fully experiencing or understanding its surroundings.

For all philosophy that equates psychic life with self-awareness (that is to say, for every philosophical system until Hegel), it is impossible to admit unconscious phenomena. That unconscious psychic events should infiltrate the ego behind its back, so to speak, influence its decisions, and restrict its (supposed) autonomy amounts to a grave affront to mankind's self-image. Freud himself remarked as much when he qualified his discovery as one of the three great injuries to human narcissism that have occurred in history. These affronts are Copernicus's *cosmological* vision, Darwin's *biological* theory, and Freud's own *psychological* notions.[23] All three insults to received ideas have had a *decentering* effect. With Copernicus, the earth is removed from the center of the universe; Darwin deprives man of his special place in creation; and Freud makes consciousness an epiphenomenon of the psyche. As Freud writes, the ego is "not master in its own house," even though it deceives itself through the narcissistic illusion it maintains by affirming "I think." We will encounter the Freudian movement of *decentering* in the works of Derrida, who challenges the (self-)deception of logocentrism and Eurocentrism in his works.

Freud was not a philosopher. He wanted psychoanalysis to be accepted as a strict science (as is evident when he compared himself to Copernicus and Darwin). His *decentering* of the subject was anticipated not by Heidegger, who was twenty-three years his junior, but by Nietzsche and, to a lesser extent, by Schopenhauer.[24] To Freud's own list of theories that contested man's self-image, we should therefore add the *philosophical* inquisitions of Nietzsche, whose "guesses and intuitions," Freud wrote, "often agree in the most astonishing way with the laborious findings of psychoanalysis."[25] Even more than Heidegger and Freud, Nietzsche stands for the "end of metaphysics"—not just the "death of God" he famously announced, but the death of the human subject, as well. Nietzsche's genealogical critique of reason anticipates deconstruction in many ways. "When I analyze the process that is expressed in the sentence, 'I think,'" Nietzsche writes in *Beyond Good and Evil*,

I find a whole series of daring assertions that would be difficult, perhaps impossible, to prove; for example, that it is *I* who think (1), that there must necessarily be something that thinks (2), that thinking is an activity and operation on the part of a being who is thought of as a cause (3), that there is an "ego" (4), and, finally, that it is already determined what is to be designated by thinking (5)— that I *know* what thinking is (6).[26]

Here, in abbreviated and condensed form, Nietzsche casts doubt on an array of basic philosophical concepts: consciousness (1), substance (2), causality (3), the subject (4), the referentiality of language (5), and knowledge/insight (6). Nietzsche denies that the little sentence, "I think," rests upon a secure foundation or possesses any degree of certainty; instead, its basis is provided by "daring assertions" and "the superstitions of logicians." In opposition, he sets forth "a small terse fact":

namely, that a thought comes when "it" wishes, and not when "I" wish, so that it is a falsification of the facts of the case to say that the subject "I" is the condition of the predicate "think." *It* thinks; but that this "it" is precisely the famous old "ego" is, to put it mildly, only a supposition, an assertion, and assuredly not an "immediate certainty."[27]

Through the mediation of Georg Groddeck, this passage inspired Freud's second model of the psychic apparatus, which posited the division of the mind into ego, id, and super-ego.

Nietzsche was also the first to have declared occidental culture's loss of faith in its highest values "nihilism." Absurdly, to this very day, he is often called a "nihilist" himself for supposedly being their *destroyer* (a criticism that, in the twentieth century, was also leveled at deconstruction and poststructuralism). For Nietzsche, however, "nihilism" is just as little a call to active demolition as Heidegger's "destruction of metaphysics" or Derrida's deconstruction. Instead, it represents, more than anything else, a diagnosis: Nietzsche is referring to the fact that "the highest values have devalued themselves." Thereby, he sums up a condition of culture and history in which faith in the Christian God as the guarantor of truth and morality has vanished—to say nothing of the belief in universal morals and the objectivity of human knowledge. This diagnosis proposes to change the task of philosophy: instead of seeking to deduce the rules of morality and knowledge from universal principles, the questions it raises are historical—or, to use Nietzsche's own term, *genealogical*. Nietzsche's philosophical genealogy does not ask for an absolute *origin*, but for historical *background* and *provenance*, as well as for the psychological basis of values and their opposites. Thus, it is not concerned with determining how we can reliably and "objectively" discern good and evil, true and false, right and wrong, and so on (questions it abandons as unanswerable), but rather *how it happens* that we distinguish—and have distinguished—between good and evil, true and false, and so on, *in this way and not otherwise*.

The focus no longer falls on either side of a distinction or its onto-logical value, but is directed *toward* the *act of differentiation/distinction itself* as a way of *creating* values that is also, at the same time, a historically contingent operation. As Nietzsche puts it in the *Genealogy of Morals*:

We need a *critique* of moral values, *the value of these values themselves must first be called in question*—and for that there is needed a knowledge of the conditions and circumstances in which they grew, under which they evolved and changed (morality as consequence, as symptom, as mask, as tartufferie, as illness, as mis-understanding; but also morality as cause, as remedy, as stimulant, as restraint, as poison), a knowledge of a kind that has never yet existed or even been desired.[28]

The question concerning the "value of values" therefore already implies that "the Good," "the True," "the Beautiful," and so on, do not have their value "in themselves" but are instead matters of value-judgment that have been established in a certain way, and not otherwise. Thus, for example, "the judgment 'good' did *not*," according to Nietzsche,

originate with those to whom "goodness" was shown! Rather, it was "the good" themselves, that is to say, the noble, powerful, high-stationed and high-minded, who felt and established themselves and their actions as good, that is, of the first rank, in contradistinction to all the low, low-minded, common and plebeian. It was out of this *pathos of distance* that they first seized the right to create values and to coin names for values: what had they to do with utility! [. . .] (The lordly right of giving names extends so far that one should allow oneself to conceive the origin of language itself as an expression of power on the part of rulers: they say "this *is* this and this," they seal every thing and event with a sound and, as it were, take possession of it.)[29]

As later occurred in the works of Heidegger, the *form of judgment* itself is subject to scrutiny, even though Nietzsche shows less concern for the Being that undergoes judgment than for the performative power of the act of judging, which does not trade in representations of the world so much as it creates the world by making determinations about good and evil, truth and lie, light and shadow, value and its opposite in certain ways—and not differently.

It is worth stressing that the guiding distinctions, around which the West has organized its philosophical systems, never consist of two parts of the same value. One must, as Derrida puts it, "recognize that in a classi-cal philosophical opposition we are not dealing with the peaceful coexis-tence of a *vis-à-vis*, but rather with a violent hierarchy."[30] One of the two terms governs the other and stands above it: the true above the false, good above evil, light above shadow, being above nothing, right above wrong, spirit above body, reason above the senses, the signified above the signifier, identity above difference, man above woman, etc. The hierarchical relationship that governs a given pair of terms posits that one of the two parts is original and central, whereas the other is derivative and marginal. (Here, Being once again comes into play, as the centrality of privileged terms is always interpreted as being ontologically more complete.) If the inaugural gesture of deconstruction entails reversing the hierarchy of such oppositions (above all, the one between voice and writing, cf. Chapter 2), Nietzsche already observes that both sides of a given distinction also communicate with each other in a subterranean fashion, so to speak. In genealogical terms, what *language* makes appear to be a matter of either/or does not really obtain:

For all the value that the true, the truthful, the selfless may deserve, it would still be possible that a higher and more fundamental value for life might have to be ascribed to deception, selfishness, and lust. It might even be possible that what constitutes the value of these good and revered things is precisely that they are insidiously related, tied to, and involved with these wicked, seemingly opposite things—maybe even one with them in essence.[31]

Therefore, it is due only to our fundamental forgetting or repression of the *origin* of our value judgments that we have come to believe in oppositions between values as something absolute. By uncovering the source of value judgments, genealogy destroys belief—which it can do only because belief in the truth has long since undermined itself.

The *genealogical* or *archeological* gesture of uncovering forgotten origins and repressed pasts that one encounters, in different forms, in the works of Nietzsche, Heidegger, and Freud, is also to be found in Derrida. It is no coincidence that this genealogical gesture connects with a new way of thinking about language that developed around 1900, to which we now turn in concluding our introductory chapter.

1.4 The Crisis of Language, the Linguistic Turn, and Structuralism (Saussure)

Already for Nietzsche, the search for the derivation of metaphysical concepts and values entails a thorough critique of language as the medium of insight and knowledge. Grammar, according to Nietzsche, structures our perception of reality. Because language offers us subjects and objects, actors and action, Being and Becoming, we believe that these things are also a natural part of reality, whereas in fact we only project grammatical categories and linguistic representations (including those of the "thing" itself) onto the outside world. "We set up a word at the point at which our ignorance begins, at which we can see no further," Nietzsche wrote in an unpublished aphorism from the 1880s, "e.g., the word 'I,' the word 'do,' the word 'suffer':—these are perhaps the horizon of our knowledge, but not 'truths.'"[32] At the same time, Nietzsche also notes the inescapability of this linguistic and perspectival distortion: *"We cease to think when we refuse to do so under the constraint of language;* we barely reach the doubt that sees this limitation as a limitation. *Rational thought is interpretation according to a scheme that we cannot throw off,"*[33] he writes in the same passage. Along similar lines, Derrida observed some hundred years later in "Structure, Sign and Play in the Discourse of the Human Sciences": "There is no sense in doing without the concepts of metaphysics in order to shake metaphysics. We have no language—no syntax and no lexicon—which is foreign to this history; we can pronounce not a single destructive proposition which has not already had to slip into the form, the logic, and the implicit postulations of precisely what it seeks to contest."[34]

Language—in its grammatical structures and categories, as well as the systems of thought that are built upon them—is no longer conceived in terms of insight, knowledge, or the representation of the world, but as a kind of screen or filter that stands between its users and material reality, something that shapes our access to the world while distorting it at the same time. Since around 1900, the *linguistic skepticism* in evidence here has provided a key focus for philosophical and poetic reflection. Hugo von Hofmannsthal's *Chandos Letter* provides a prime example. "In brief, this is my case: I have completely lost the ability to think or speak coherently about anything at all." "I felt an inexplicable uneasiness in even pronouncing the words 'spirit,' 'soul,' or 'body,'" the *Letter* continues, "for the abstract words which the tongue must enlist as a matter of course in order to bring out an opinion disintegrate in my mouth like rotten mushrooms."[35] Independent of contemporary philosophical and literary developments, Ferdinand de Saussure, who is generally considered the founder of structuralism, came to the same conclusion in his linguistic theory. All these events form part of the so-called "linguistic turn," which occurred at the beginning of the twentieth century—a paradigm shift that affected the whole of the humanities and placed new emphasis on the phenomenon of language as a way not so much of depicting reality as of producing it.

Saussure himself demonstrated little interest in the consequences of his conception of language for philosophical epistemology. His aim was to establish linguistics as a positive science. However, the consequences of his theory for the humanities—ethnology, psychoanalysis, literary studies, and philosophy (including deconstruction)—were so fundamental that the basic ideas must be enumerated before we can proceed to a discussion of Derrida's *Of Grammatology* (which critiques and expands what Saussure began).

It is worth stressing that the originality of Saussure's approach does not lie in his thesis that the linguistic sign is arbitrary. This idea is as old as thought about language itself and can already be found in Aristotle. "Spoken sounds," we read in *De Interpretatione*,

Are symbols of affections in the soul, and written marks symbols of spoken sounds. And just as written marks are not the same for all men, neither are spoken sounds. But what these are in the first place signs of—affections of the soul—are the same for all; and what these affections are likenesses of—actual things—are also the same.[36]

In Saussure's terminology (which in turn connects with the lexicon of scholasticism), the "affections in the soul" (or mental representations) are called the *signified* (in a scholastic phrasing: *signatum*), and sounds and graphic marks are called the *signifier (signans)*. What Aristotle and, after him, the scholastics formulated is a (indeed, *the*) classic *representational theory* of language; this conception of language continued, in different forms, until Hegel. According to this theory, what is signified (that is, mental representation) involves the natural depiction of objects, and these objects are the same for all people. Only in a second step is signified matter designated by signifiers (i.e., spoken and written words). In contrast to what is signified, signifiers are arbitrary, for different languages qualify the same idea (e.g., "tree") by means of different combinations of sounds and letters (*Baum, arbor, arbre,* etc.). Signifieds are natural representations of things; verbal signifiers (spoken words) are artificial and conventional representations of signifieds. Signifiers in writing (letters), in turn, are artificial and conventional representations of verbal expressions and therefore "of the second order." Such a gradated scheme of representations also establishes an ontological hierarchy inasmuch as, along with distance from the "things themselves," the power of representation and, therefore, the quotient of "reality" diminishes, as it were: signifieds possess fullness, for they (supposedly) consist of pre-linguistic impressions made by objects directly on the mind; spoken words involve a step away from direct reference to reality, but their proximity to mental representations, through the consciousness of the speaker who voices them, still assures relative accuracy; finally, written signs are "merely" signs of spoken words—signifers of signifiers, that is—and, because they are cut off from the consciousness of the speaker, they stand at the farthest remove from the living, embodied truth of the speaker.

Aristotle—and the whole tradition after him—conceives of language in terms of *meaning* (the signified), *reference* (material objects), and, ultimately, *representation* (a sign standing for, and depicting, a thing). Because it is an arbitrary and conventional system of signs, language, as the *medium of access to the world*, is exposed to error and misinterpretation, but, because its users remain oriented in a reality they share with others through consciousness and intention, its fundamental reliability prevails. Still more: through the equation "*one* object for *one* representation for *one* signifier (per language)," it also seems assured that the divisions of language correspond to the division of things. While one can err and, at a distance, mistake a dog for a cat, or (as in the Greek legend of the grapes of Zeuxis) confuse painted grapes for real ones, there can be no doubt that dogs, cats, grapes, and pictures of grapes really exist—and that these things exist fully as entities inherently different from one another and identical to themselves in terms of their fundamental essence. In the classical theory of language as representation, reference to reality—and therefore the "truthfulness" of language and the distinctions constituting it—is guaranteed.[37]

Saussure's linguistics intervenes at the decisive juncture of semiotics, epistemology, and ontology. As mentioned, this does not occur explicitly, but follows from his conception of the linguistic sign—or, more precisely, from the changed position of the *signified* within his theory. To state matters in summary fashion: *for Saussure, signifieds are parts of the linguistic sign—they are just as arbitrary and conventional as signifiers. In this view, they cease to be natural representations of things and become effects of signification instead. Consequently, Saussure questions language's reference to reality in a more fundamental way than anyone before him.* The equation between *one* object and *one* representation loses its validity; as a result, the distinctions made in language no longer qualify as an adequate representation of "the order of things." If, for classical theories of the sign, the identity of the individual sign was guaranteed by its reference to the signified (and thus, ultimately, by the self-identity of its referent in reality), for Saussure, the question is how the internal divisions of language (i.e., the differences between signifiers and signifieds alike) have come to be at all. His answer is that it has occurred through *articulation* (and not *representation*). This response seems straightforward, but it requires some additional commentary insofar as the principle of *articulation* leads to the concept of language as a *system of differences* (and not identities). Herein lies the truly revolutionary aspect of Saussure's linguistics.

Saussure's point of departure is that both the sonic and ideational materials of language (potential signifiers and signifieds, that is) are initially present to human consciousness only as two amorphous masses without inherent divisions. A "chaotic mass of representations" is paired with an equally undifferentiated array of sounds that neither mean nor refer to anything by themselves. Only in the process of articulation—in French, *articuler* means both "to voice" and "to divide/distribute"—do recognizable signifiers and signifieds emerge. *Language as articulation does not stem from a pre-ordained presence (of meaning or of reality); rather, it is determined by a process of differentiation that produces identities only after the fact, as effects:*

The characteristic role of language with respect to thought is not to create a material, phonic means for expressing ideas but to serve as a link between thought and sound, under conditions that of necessity bring about the reciprocal delimitations of units. Thought, chaotic by nature, has to become ordered in the process of its decomposition. Neither are thoughts given material form nor are sounds transformed into mental entities; the somewhat mysterious fact is rather that "thought-sound" implies division, and that language works out its units while taking shape between two shapeless masses. [. . .]

Language might be called the domain of articulations [. . .]. Each linguistic term is a member, an *articulus* in which an idea is fixed in a sound and a sound becomes the sign of an idea.[38]

Therefore, it is impossible to treat language as "a naming-process only"—that is, as Saussure writes, as "a list of words, each corresponding to the thing that it names."[39] This conception of language presumes "that ready-made ideas exist before words."[40] Instead, Saussure describes language as a system of *values* in which the meaning of the signs can only be determined through their difference from, and opposition to, other signs.

Saussure illustrates his claim by comparing words and money. To determine the value of a five-Euro bill, for example, one must not only know what quantity of another thing it can be exchanged for (bread, for instance); one must also compare it to a similar value in the same system (e.g., a one-Euro coin) or to a unit from another system (e.g., a five-dollar bill):

In the same way, a word can be exchanged for something dissimilar, an idea; besides, it can be compared with something of the same nature, another word. Its value is therefore not fixed so long as one simply states that it can be "exchanged" for a given concept, i.e. that it has this or that signification: one must also compare it with similar values, with other words that stand in opposition to it. *Its content is really fixed only by the concurrence of everything that exists outside it.*[41]

Thus, the French *mouton* can have the same meaning as the English word *sheep*—the animal one finds on a meadow—but it cannot possess the same *value*. The same animal, when one encounters it in a stew, is no longer called "sheep," but "mutton," whereas French only has one word for both ideas. In more general terms:

Instead of pre-existing ideas then, we find in all the foregoing examples *values* emanating from the system. When they are said to correspond to concepts, it is understood that the concepts are purely differential and defined not by their positive content but negatively by their relations with the other terms of the system. *Their most precise characteristic is in being what the others are not.* [. . .]

Everything that has been said up to this point boils down to this: in language, there are only differences. Even more important: a difference generally implies positive terms between which the difference is set up; but in language there are only differences without positive terms.[42]

For Saussure, differences do not exist between pre-constituted identities. Rather, it is the other way around: identities only emerge retroactively, from the process of *articulation* of differences, and therefore they are never stable. With this principle, Saussure transformed linguistics into a field concerned with the *thinking of the non-identical*—a terrain where the humanities of the twentieth century were to meet up, whether they received their inspiration directly from Saussure and structuralism or not.

Despite the many divergences between Heidegger's determination of Dasein as "between," the psychoanalytic concept of the divided subject, Adorno's negative dialectics, Levinas's phenomenology of the Other, and Derrida's radicalized thinking of *différance—all these projects share the common denominator of critiquing the principle of identity as the logical, ontological, cultural, and political norm of the ways we think and act.* In this critique, the "transvaluation of all values" that Nietzsche predicted is taking place inasmuch as the side of classical distinctions privileged by tradition—identity over difference, the same over the other, presence over absence, position over negation, being over non-being, etc.—loses its preeminence and, as in Saussure's linguistic theory, is made to appear dependent on its opposite. This is not just a matter of logical or academic games, but has eminent cultural and political consequences. If, today, it seems self-evident to us (or, at any rate, to some or many of us), that sexual identity does not follow from a preordained "essence" of Woman or Man, or that cultural identity is not rooted in the natural substance of the blood or national spirit, but that these and other identities, to the extent that they allow themselves to be stabilized at all, are inevitably suffused with differences—which constitute them and thereby reveal them to be internally divided and non-identical at their core—this has occurred thanks not least to the process of which Saussure forms an exemplary part. Deconstruction, whose specific features we will turn to in a moment, has also contributed to this process.

Before moving on, we should cast a brief glance at structuralism, which invokes Saussure as its founder. Saussure himself did not employ the expressions "structure" or "structuralism"; as mentioned, he spoke of language as a "system of differences." However, one already finds in his works the idea that the differential—or, as it has increasingly been called since the 1930s, the "structural"—way of looking is not limited to verbal language. As a "social institution," we read in the *Course*, language is comparable to other practices—for example, writing, sign language, symbolic rites, forms of courtesy, and military signals; in general, customs and conventions can be understood as sign systems. Thus, linguistics in the narrower sense forms part of a general science of signs, for which Saussure proposed the name *semiology*.[43] Structuralism takes up this mode of thinking and describes extra-linguistic objects as languages: systems of kinship (Claude Lévi-Strauss), the unconscious (Jacques Lacan), fashion, eating, and sports (Roland Barthes), common sense (Clifford Geertz)—indeed, culture in its entirety comes under the lens. Thereby, the guiding principle remains Saussure's notion that a single phenomenon (e.g., the prohibition of incest, cross-cousin marriage, or certain table manners) can never be understood in isolation, but must be examined in terms of *a role or function in a system*, which theory has the task of recognizing and describing.

Since cultural systems are necessarily social, but essentially unconscious (a feature of language, as Saussure already observed), it is not enough to ask the social actors about the "deep grammar" of a given practice—to inquire directly, that is, about the meaning of this or that phenomenon in particular. Instead, it is necessary to possess a special analytic means of investigation to "distill" the structure in question. As far as these special means of investigation are concerned, structuralism is still guided by linguistics, and especially by phonology, which developed the method of the so-called "minimal pair analysis" in order to determine basic units of sound (or phonemes) that, within a given language, allow for the creation of meaning. In minimal pairs like "ban—man" or "house—mouse," for example, the initial sounds (b/m and h/m) serve the sole purpose of *distinguishing* these words; such sounds mark points of differentiation, which establish the building blocks of meaning. Likewise, structuralists look for "minimal pairs of kinship," "mythemes," "vestemes," etc., as basic units whose differential organization yields a socially valid ensemble. Thus, according to Roland Barthes, the structuralist method consists primarily of finding oppositions that organize a given cultural formation (e.g., habits of eating, ways of dressing, literary texts, rites, symphonies, and the like). This analytical tool for ascertaining oppositions that create meaning can also be employed on a larger scale: the raw and the cooked, nature and culture, "savage" and "civilized" ways of thinking, composure and affect—the series could be continued at will.

In the structuralist reduction of general *differentiality* to *pairs of opposition*, however, the binary scheme of metaphysics resurfaces. Often, it is difficult to determine the status of oppositional pairs in structural analyses: is it "only" a matter of guiding analytical distinctions, or are these distinctions ascribed ontological value? As for the concept of the sign itself that underlies the structuralist enterprise: does the distinction between signifier and signified not continue the history of metaphysics, too? Is this division desirable? Necessary? Inevitable? How, if we can no longer believe in the truthfulness of the distinctions we make, can we arrive at judgments at all? Will our experience be like that of Lord Chandos, for whom all linguistic distinctions "which the tongue must enlist as a matter of course in order to bring out an opinion" disintegrate in our mouths "like rotten mushrooms"? Is this the end of philosophy? Might we then, finally, learn how to live? With these questions in mind, we now turn to the writings of Derrida.

Second Approach: The Metaphysics of Presence and the Deconstruction of Logocentrism

> I cannot explain what deconstruction is to me without putting matters in context. At the time that, under this title, I undertook my task, structuralism was predominant. Deconstruction staked out a position against structuralism. On the other hand, it was a time when scientific theories of language governed everything, references to linguistics, "all things are a language." At the time—I'm speaking of the 1960s—deconstruction began to take shape as . . . I wouldn't say as "anti-structuralism," but, all the same, by taking a certain distance from structuralism and casting the authority of language into doubt.
>
> Therefore, it astonishes and irritates me in equal measure every time that deconstruction (as commonly occurs) is equated with—how should I put it?— "omnilingualism," "panlingualism," or "pantextualism." Deconstruction starts with just the opposite. I began by contesting the authority of linguistics, language, and logocentrism.[1]

2.1 Speech and Writing (*Grammatology*)

In 1967, three books appeared simultaneously which established the philosophical program of deconstruction. The first is *Speech and Phenomena: An Essay on the Problem of the Sign in Husserl's Philosophy.* The second is *Of Grammatology*, which remains—still today—Derrida's best-known and possibly most important work. The third is *Writing and Difference*, a collection of essays in which Derrida engages critically with structuralism. Derrida followed these works with *Margins of Philosophy*, also a collection of essays, and *Dissemination*, a series of interrelated texts about Plato, Stéphane Mallarmé, and Philippe Sollers. These two books, which were published in France in 1972, elaborate the critique of logocentrism set forth in *Grammatology*.

Before we turn to the terms that are important for Derrida—phonocentrism, Eurocentrism, writing, trace, *différance*, and play—a few general observations are in order.

When one looks at the indexes of the aforementioned books, two things are immediately apparent. First, the program of deconstruction unfolds almost entirely in the form of *readings*. Deconstruction is both a philosophical project and a *practice of reading*. Second, these readings are not restricted to the canon of philosophy and related fields; just as often, they involve *literary* texts. Alongside essays on Plato, Hegel, Heidegger, Nietzsche, Freud, Saussure, J. L. Austin, Levinas, and others, Derrida analyzes the writings of Edmond Jabès, Antonin Artaud, Mallarmé, Maurice Blanchot, Paul Valéry, and Philippe Sollers. The latter half of *Grammatology* explores Rousseau, who wrote both theoretical and literary texts; for Derrida, the *Confessions* and *Émile* are just as important and rich in theoretical implications as is Rousseau's *Essay on the Origin of Languages*, the main object of analysis in *Grammatology*. This methodological combination—the significance of *reading* across lines of genre in deconstructive praxis— is, without a doubt, a key reason why Derrida's works met with favorable reception among European and American scholars of literature before they were embraced by academic philosophers (a situation that still holds true in part). The institutional history of deconstruction illustrates how *reading*, in a sense requiring more detailed explication, is an altogether philosophical activity for Derrida—indeed, it may be said to represent *the* exemplary mode of philosophical engagement, period.

For Derrida—as for Nietzsche, and Heidegger before him—reading (which also means *writing* the reading one performs) entails the responsibility of engaging critically with metaphysical inheritance; just as it cannot be viewed as a fixed acquisition, metaphysics cannot be rejected out of hand. No one, with a similar degree of penetration or with greater frequency, has emphasized that we *are inheritors* of the past—that the foundation of our *Being*, here and today, does not rest secure in nature, but instead belongs to a tradition that we can as little deny as simply capitalize upon. This inheritance remains bequeathed to us, and we must draw on it, whether we want to or not (and whether we do so knowingly or not). In contrast to Foucault and Deleuze—and in contradistinction, also, to the unbridled individualism of so-called "postmodernism"—Derrida always insisted that it is not enough to come up with new names, to assign new values to old concepts, or to declare the "end" of this or that (be it history, metaphysics, patriarchy, or anything else) in order to escape the *structure of the inheritance.* Derrida's caveat from *Writing and Difference* cannot be repeated often enough: "We have no language—no syntax and no lexicon—which is foreign to this history; we can pronounce not a single destructive proposition which has not already had to slip into the form, the logic, and the implicit postulations of precisely what it seeks to contest."[2]

This oppositional pairing of having to resign oneself (to the philosophical idiom that has been passed down—its syntax, lexicon, and the history of its operative distinctions) and wanting to put into question this same inheritance determines deconstructive reading (and writing) as an operation that is equally *genealogical* and *strategic.* It is *genealogical,* because—after Nietzsche, Heidegger, and Freud—it means uncovering the forgotten pre-history of a grand philosophical tradition and exposing its assumptions, the places where its blind spots lie. It is *strategic* because this is only possible by means of a double rhetorical gesture, which on the one hand *reverses* prevailing distinctions, and on the other (for a mere upending of received ideas is not enough) tries to displace key concepts in order to bring the text of tradition into motion in a specific way—opening it up and pushing it beyond itself. A look at *Grammatology* will illustrate this practice of reading.

Grammatology is still wholly classical in design: the first part, "Writing before the Letter," outlines a theoretical position that is "put to the test"[3] in the second part, "Nature, Culture, Writing" (even if Rousseau's *Essay on the Origin of Languages* no longer counts, strictly speaking, as a "case study," and the "Age of Rousseau"—that is, the eighteenth century—turns out to be a threshold-moment for the modern crisis of writing). In the twentieth century, Derrida claims, the crisis of writing assumes the form of a return of the repressed: the return of writing which begins to abandon its inherited position as a "signifier of the second order" (i.e., its status as a derivative and inferior representation of spoken words) and, increasingly, comes to encompass the whole of linguistic activity. In this light, the so-called *linguistic turn*, in the wake of which the humanities finally came to determine as language the totality of their problematic horizon,[4] itself represents nothing but a symptom of this return.

But what does it mean, when discussing the history of metaphysics and the determination of Being as presence, to speak of the "repression" of writing and its "return"? Despite the Freudian vocabulary he employs, Derrida makes it clear that it does not involve performing a psychoanalytic interpretation of philosophy.[5] Indeed, psychoanalysis itself still belongs to the epoch of "logocentric oppression," even though, at the same time, it opens a way out.

We already have seen (cf. above, 1.4) that, for the metaphysical tradition since Aristotle, spoken words—which are proximate to meaning and to the intention of the speaker—count as primary signifiers, whereas writing has received the secondary and subordinate function of representing spoken words (that is, of being the signifier of other signifiers). It is this devaluation of writing with respect to speech and the voice that Derrida calls "repression." Why, however, does he employ this "strong" word for a classification that seems purely technical—a pragmatic matter of classifying and ordering different forms of linguistic signs? In fact, repression does not simply mean pushing something aside or declaring it less important than other matters. On the contrary, it means defending against the offending matter and excluding it from consciousness because it poses a danger and threatens the integrity of the psyche. What is so menacing about writing that it must be repressed—shut out from what is thought to constitute the essence of language and locked into the cultural unconscious? Or, put somewhat differently: what consciousness, what claims, what cultural illusions does this exclusion defend?

One answer may be found in Plato's *Phaedrus*:

SOCRATES: You know, Phaedrus, writing shares a strange feature with painting. The offsprings of painting stand there as if they are alive, but if anyone asks them anything, they remain most solemnly silent. The same is true of written words. You'd think they were speaking as if they had some understanding, but if you question anything that has been said because you want to learn more, it continues to signify just that very same thing forever. When it has once been written down, every discourse roams about everywhere, reaching indiscriminately those with understanding no less than those who have no business with it, and it doesn't know to whom it should speak and to whom it should not. And when it is faulted and attacked unfairly, it always needs its father's support; alone, it can neither defend itself nor come to its own support.[6]

Writing, one can see, represents "fatherless" speech. In contrast to the spoken word, it can be separated from the body and the consciousness of its originator; without a master, it wanders alone in the world. It is impossible to foresee into whose hands it will fall and what effects it will produce without the assistance of its author. Since writing arrives without commentary or context, it is exposed to misinterpretation and misunderstanding. One can do what one wants with written words: their meaning dissolves into multiple, competing interpretations. What's more, writing—like painting—is suffused with false vitality. Its deceptive nature misleads the reader, who thinks he understands it as well as the spoken words it imitates. In fact, without the possibility of checking with the author himself, one can miss his intention by miles and not even notice. In fine, writing is afflicted with absence: absence of intentional consciousness, absence of objects, and absence of meaning.[7]

Of course, the perils inherent in writing are familiar to every literary scholar as the problem of "hermeneutic difference," or, alternately, "hermeneutic distance." Until approximately the middle of the twentieth century, philological methods of interpretation sought only to bridge this gap and, by reconstructing what the author originally intended, to reestablish the complete presence of meaning in the text by sublating the "false" vitality of the letters into the "true" life of the mind. However, behind this hierarchical order that sets the voice above writing, the presence of meaning above its absence, and the spirit above the letter, lies the unquestioned assumption that the spoken word really stands beyond all the deficiencies of writing—that *phone* (voice) and *logos* (reason, meaning) comprise a unity in which the absences and "defects" of writing are collected and transformed into so many presences.

What would it mean if it were revealed that the Western conception of language, based as it is on phono- and logocentrism, is an illusion? What if spoken words, like written ones, were not animated by the intention of speakers and, instead, lacked fullness and presence? What if spoken words were not signifiers of the signified but also signifiers of other signifiers and thus themselves a kind of "writing"? This is the claim set forward in *Grammatology*, which Derrida details in the book's first part. Writing (as what the Western understanding of language has "repressed") turns out not to be what it has conventionally been taken for—a system of notation of secondary importance—but rather, in a sense that requires further explication, a feature of spoken language itself. Writing is "repressed" to uphold the illusions of logocentrism. Derrida first identified this structure in *Speech and Phenomena: An Essay on the Problem of the Sign in Husserl's Philosophy*. In the most basic terms, it involves a physiological state of affairs: when I speak, I hear myself speaking. I can hear my own voice, which issues from my mouth and, at the same time, passes back inside through the ears. Irrespective of the fact that others may be present and listening, my body always finds itself in a circuit closed upon itself. According to Husserl—who, on this point, stands in for a long philosophical tradition—speaking invariably consists of the intentional expression of meaning. This meaning (Saussure's signified) lies ready within consciousness and is then performed or realized in the act of speech; it exteriorizes itself by passing into the voice (articulate sounds, or signifiers). Inasmuch as I can hear myself speak, I always (seem to) revoke this exteriorization even as I perform it: I take the meaning back into the interiority of my consciousness, which is revealed, by virtue of this same process, as self-consciousness. *Logos* sounds forth in *phonè*; at the same time, *phonè* is constituted by *logos* listening to itself. Therefore, self-consciousness, the state of being present-to-oneself, implies the self-sufficiency of ideal interiority coupled in a feedback loop with the signified. According to Derrida, the metaphysics of presence has its foundation ("absolute proximity of voice and being, of voice and the meaning of being, of voice and the ideality of meaning"[8]) in this narcissistic illusion—a kind of "acoustic mirror stage"—of self-consciousness that is present to itself and its intentions. Enclosed within the circle of pure self-reference, the subject deems itself its own master, the master of meaning, and master of the objects, since, as we have seen, meanings or "symbols of affections in the soul" count for the Aristotelian tradition as natural images of the things themselves (that is, as a kind of pre-linguistic universal language). In this perspective, the self-assurance of the subject, the self-presentation of its representations, and, through them, the power to grasp and to manipulate the objects of the world are one and the same thing.

In *Grammatology*, Derrida contests this philosophical position and the hierarchically arranged values that follow from it: the privileging of interiority above exteriority, of ideality above materiality, of the intelligible above the sensible, of time above space, of presence above absence, and so on. Writing, however, instantiates all these "problems": the medium of self-forgetting and distraction, it is at once something exterior, material, and spatial—the opposite of interiority and the opposite of memory (*Erinnerung*) upon which the spirit (*Geist*) and its history rely. Without interruption, the philosophical tradition from Plato to Hegel has distrusted writing and praised the "living spirit" (as the first chapter of *Grammatology* richly documents). The same value judgment is found in Saussure. "Language and writing are two distinct systems of signs; the second exists for the sole purpose of representing the first,"[9] one reads in the *Course*. The objective of linguistics follows: "The linguistic object is not both the written and the spoken forms of words; the spoken forms alone constitute the object."[10] Following Saussure, linguistics has adhered to this definition and developed phonetics and phonology—and not graphemics and grammatology. Structuralism, too, is modeled on phonology.

The objective of *Speech and Phenomena* is to demonstrate that, as an *operation of the voice*, the "I-me" of (seemingly) pure auto-affection is in fact predicated on a difference that breaks apart the unity of affecting and being affected. This is the case, in the first place, because hearing oneself speak contains a minimal temporal interval between speaking and hearing. Secondly, even interior monologue (Husserl's favorite example when discussing auto-affection) requires one to use signifiers and therefore necessitates *articulation* (in Saussure's sense of the word), which interrupts the presumed immediacy of meaning and consciousness. As soon as one grants—as Husserl does—that self-consciousness rests upon auto-affection, which in turn depends on articulation, "I" and "me" no longer form a complete unity. Even in the mute state of being alone with oneself (or being alone with one's thoughts), a foundational difference is at work. Still more: without this difference in place, neither self-awareness nor self-experience would be possible at all—it is only through interruption that the circuit can be closed. In this sense, "pure" self-consciousness represents an impossibility, a tautology, the awareness of nothing. Derrida writes:

> This movement of *différance* is not something that happens to a transcendental subject; it produces a subject. Auto-affection is not a modality of experience that characterizes a being that would already be itself (*autos*). It produces sameness as self-relation within self-difference; it produces sameness as the nonidentical.[11]

Through the opening produced by this difference, the aperture that takes place within the ego itself, everything again comes into play that was thought to have been excluded from the hermetic circuit of auto-affection: space, the exterior, the body, absence, and death.

Therefore, even within the history of metaphysics, the status of the voice is ambivalent. On the one hand, from Plato to Hegel, it is conceived as the medium of pure interiority and ideal meanings—as something that is almost nothing in terms of materiality (which has already vanished at the very moment it appears). "My words are 'alive' because they seem not to leave me: not to fall outside me, outside my breath, at a visible distance; [they seem] not to cease to belong to me, to be at my disposition."[12] Yet at the same time, the voice remains a *medium*, a *passageway*, which interrupts the integral state of meaning being present. "Why can the living spirit not appear before the spirit! / When the soul *speaks*, alas, it is no longer the *soul* that speaks!" Schiller's plaintive distich in the *Xenien* gives vivid expression to the conflict within the voice, even as it articulates the ideal of direct, unmediated communication; this ideal remains inseparably bound to the experience of *belatedness* or *secondariness*: *first,* there are representations in the soul, and *only then* does their expression or articulation occur. For Derrida, in contrast—and *after* Saussure—thought grapples with the *primal condition of mediation* that affects our mental images.

Husserl plays only a subordinate role in *Grammatology* (even though *Speech and Phenomena* in many senses provided the basis for *Grammatology*, offering key figures of thought in this work). However, Derrida introduces and develops the notions of *différance*, trace, and original supplementarity in his reading of Husserl. In *Grammatology*, Saussure again provides a main inspiration for Derrida's figures of thought. Saussure per-petuates the phonocentric repression of writing, even though, by the same token, his radicalized conception of language as a system of differences should have (or might have) prevented such repression from occurring. Throughout his oeuvre, Derrida remains interested in the (self-)contra-dictions that escape the "intentional consciousness" of authors, which he does not interpret as defects or mistakes, but as *symptoms* of a process that reaches far beyond conscious *and even unconscious* awareness—symptoms of the return of the repressed, written into texts against the will of the authors (or at least independent of it), which wait to be decoded. (In the final instance, the same is true of Derrida's own works.)

Classically, literary and philosophical commentary have focused on resolving, as much as possible, contradictions in the work of a given author and revealing them to be matters that are not substantive—or resolving them by showing how they mark a point of development from one posi-tion to another. (Freedom from contradiction is the ideal not only of every philosophical system, but also the ideal of the self-contained work of art inasmuch as, closed upon itself, it fulfills its form.) Deconstruction, in con-trast, declares these contradictions to be of note insofar as they articulate a conflict of an epochal nature: the aforementioned conflict between having to resign oneself to the premises of tradition and the desire (or need) to think something else, which is constitutive of deconstruction itself.

Such attention to the lines of exclusion within texts—the passages where a text *does* something other than what it *says*, where something articulates itself that escapes the declared intention of its author or goes against it—is undoubtedly informed by psychoanalysis, which also does not find its way to the unconscious conflicts of the analysand through what he knows and thinks about himself, but rather through what artic-ulates itself in his words, without or against his knowledge. Neverthe-less—and this cannot be stressed often enough—deconstruction *does not represent a psychoanalytic form of textual interpretation.* That is, it does not seek to explain performative contradictions in texts by referring them to the psycho-biographical reality of an individual author: "The reading of the literary 'symptom' is most banal, most academic, most naïve."[13] More-over, instances of individual repression—the primary concern of psycho-analysis—can be properly understood only after taking account of the logocentric repression of writing—repression that, according to Derrida, commands even psychoanalytic concepts.

From the understanding of language-as-writing offered in the first part of *Grammatology*, it follows that the play of signifiers cannot be completely mastered or controlled by an author:

> The writer writes *in* a language and *in* a logic whose proper system, laws, and life his discourse by definition cannot dominate absolutely. He uses them only by letting himself, after a fashion and up to a point, be governed by the system. And the reading must always aim at a certain relationship, unperceived by the writer, between what he commands and what he does not command of the patterns of the language that he uses. This relationship is not a certain quantitative distribution of shadow and light, of weakness or of force, but a signifying structure that critical reading should *produce.*[14]

Let us now illustrate, by way of two examples—Saussure and Rousseau—what this statement means.

2.2. A Practice of Reading: The Inversion and Displacement of Concepts

The line of rejection in Saussure's text that interests Derrida—and therefore the "signifying structure" of the *Course*—emerges through the treatment writing receives. Saussure purposely and knowingly excludes writing from the field of objects addressed by linguistics (that is, he continues logocentric repression), but "around the back" and against his declared intentions, writing provides the model for language in general. Derrida's reading attempts to show that, in Saussure's conception of the linguistic sign, repressed writing returns, all efforts to banish it notwithstanding.

Saussure's exclusion of writing does not occur easily. The founder of modern linguistics seeks to make the spoken word the sole object of study, but an entire chapter at the beginning of the *Course* is devoted to cleansing, so to speak, the ideal object of the harmful influence of writing. Indeed, Saussure speaks of how language is usurped by writing. "The spoken word," one reads after the definition of linguistics quoted above,

> is so intimately bound to its written image that the latter manages to usurp the main role. People attach even more importance to the written image of a vocal sign than to

the sign itself. A similar mistake would be in thinking that more can be learned about someone by looking at his photograph than by viewing him directly.[15]

One can see that the comparison between writing and the "false vitality" of painting, already made in *Phaedrus*, is not far away. Saussure continues: "the natural and only true bond" is "the bond of sound"; "writing assumes an authority to which it has no right"; the "written image" imposes itself "at the expense of sound"; "the fact that we learn to speak before learning to write is forgotten, and the natural relation between the two is reversed."[16] For Saussure, "letting go of the letter . . . means taking a first step towards the truth."[17] (It is worth rereading these passages at length to appreciate the effort Saussure makes to counter the power assumed by writing.)

Derrida asks why Saussure exerts such effort—why does he voice almost moral indignation at the undermining of language through writing? What lies behind this affective outpouring? The answer:

the "usurpation" of which Saussure speaks, the violence by which writing would substitute itself for its own origin, for that which ought not only to have engendered it but to have been engendered from itself—such a reversal of power cannot be an accidental aberration. Usurpation necessarily refers us to a profound possibility of essence. This is without a doubt inscribed within speech itself. . . .[18]

There is an originary violence of writing because language is first, in a sense [to be revealed], writing. "Usurpation" has always already begun.[19]

The second step in Derrida's reading involves showing that Saussure himself recognizes and elaborates the original "writtenness" of language—and that he does so precisely when he no longer wishes to address the matter.

It is when he is not expressly dealing with writing, when he feels he has closed the parentheses on that subject, that Saussure opens the field of a general grammatology. Which would not only no longer be excluded from general linguistics, but would dominate it and contain it within itself. Then one realizes that what was chased off limits, the wandering outcast of linguistics, has indeed never ceased to haunt language as its primary and most intimate possibility. Then something which was never spoken and which is nothing other than writing itself as the origin of language writes itself within Saussure's discourse. [. . .] The thesis of the *arbitrariness* of the sign . . . must forbid a radical distinction between the linguistic and the graphic sign.[20]

"Writing itself as the origin of language"—needless to say (and even though the mistaken claim comes up time and again in the reception of Derrida), this is not a *historical* argument that human beings learned to read before learning to speak. Rather, the primacy or precedence of writing in relation to the spoken word means that a *structure* comes first. The differentiality of language—the absence of "positive elements" we have already remarked—makes *every* signifier, and therefore the spoken word, into the signifier of signifiers (and not of the signified). This is the condition which also makes the spoken word "fatherless" in a way: what I say or mean in a given act of speech does not depend on the intention within my consciousness, but on the system of linguistic values in which the meaning of a signifier, instead of being determined positively by its "contents," comes about negatively, through its relation to other signifiers. Consciousness does not stand at the origin of meaning; language does. Meaning does not precede articulation; instead, articulation (even if it is soundless) precedes meaning. Such a state of affairs corresponds to the classic definition of writing. In the sense—and in this sense alone—of *a field of differences that precedes every individual expression and, for the most part, escapes consciousness*, Derrida can claim that language is originally "writing," that "writing" provides the origin of language.

It is no coincidence, Derrida observes, that Saussure reintroduces writing, which he banishes at the beginning of the *Course*, in key passages about difference as the precondition of linguistic value: "Since an identical state of affairs is observable in writing, another system of signs, we shall use writing to draw some comparisons that will clarify the whole issue."[21] Four paragraphs follow that employ the example of writing exclusively and illustrate the principle of differentiality. They conclude with the sentence: "The means by which the sign is produced is completely unimportant, for it does not affect the system."[22] Thereby, "the bond of sound," which Saussure defended so vigorously against the incursions of writing, loses its status as "the only natural and true bond of language." To be sure, what is at stake in these expressions is really a "bond": the "natural bond" between signified and referent, between signifiers and signified, and, last but not least, between consciousness and "its" representations. Undoing this link is no small matter, for it means unhitching or disarticulating subject, language, and world—that is, a whole array of guiding metaphysical distinctions; indeed, the narcissistic illusion of consciousness that controls meaning and the world stands to collapse. Therefore, one can understand the effort—which Saussure is not alone in exerting—to continue thinking beyond this juncture. That is exactly what Derrida undertakes, by way of a critique that is historical and systematic at the same time.

Derrida's critique is *historical* insofar as it points out that the logocentric reduction of writing to a derivative system—a secondary representation of sounds—has only been possible within a culture of phonographic notation. In cultures that possess an ideographic or pictographic system of writing, such a reduction does not occur as easily, because the "hypothesis of representation" (i.e., the idea that every written sign represents a sound) cannot even arise—here, writing provides a system of notation that it is *independent* of the spoken word and endowed with a separate value. The first kind of writing to be entirely alphabetized developed in Greece in the fifth century BC, and the Latin alphabet still in use emerged from it subsequently. Therefore, the diffusion of phonographic writing is largely coextensive with the space of European culture, which is also where the classical theory of language-as-representation stems from. The phono- and logocentrism of Western culture entails Eurocentrism, too. The situation is not to be understood in geographical terms alone. It also means ethnocentrism and imperialism, for the culture of alphabetic writing is taken to be "inherently more intelligent" (Hegel) and superior to other systems of notation. Thus, in Rousseau's *Essay on the Origin of Languages*, one reads:

These three ways of writing correspond almost exactly to three different stages according to which one can consider men gathered into a nation. The depicting of objects is appropriate to a savage people; signs of words and of propositions, to a barbaric people; and the alphabet to civilized people.[23]

Insofar as phono- and logocentrism are tied to "Eurocentrism" and a certain geopolitical space, Derrida's project implies—it must be emphasized— a certain political critique or critique of the political. This is the case from the get-go, even if Derrida only began to address political and ethical theories explicitly in the 1990s (cf. below, Third and Fourth Approaches). With certain qualifications, Derrida's movement from the theory of signs toward open political critique represents a continuation of the inaugural gesture of deconstruction.

Derrida's critique is *systematic* insofar as it tries to reverse the binary schemes of value of phono-, logo-, and Eurocentrism, and to displace the concepts underpinning them so that they no longer conform to their metaphysical premises. To say that language was originally writing—or that writing stands at the origin of language—means reversing the classical opposition between the spoken word (voice) and writing: before the spoken word can signify anything at all, "writing" must always already have existed. At the same time, the reversal modifies the concept of writing, which Derrida no longer uses in the traditional sense of a (secondary) graphic sign-system; now, it is employed independent of the material production of signs and designates the structure of differential articulations as such. It is tempting to call this use of the concept of writing "metaphorical" (a quality hinted at inasmuch as the word appears in quotation marks) and, thereby, to distinguish the term from the way it is "literally" and "properly" used by convention. However, this does not go far enough. As we will see, Derrida's displacement of the concept of writing also collapses the distinction between "authentic" and "inauthentic" speech, between concept and metaphor.

To say that "only" metaphor stands at issue (for the opposition between concept and metaphor perpetuates the devalorization of the "inauthentic," as opposed to the "authentic") would mean declaring deconstruction itself to be merely a secondary, "inauthentic" operation that belongs to the established system of phono- and logocentric distinctions and is unable to challenge it in a substantive fashion. Instead, the point is to take the (seeming) metaphor seriously in order to see what happens when a key element upon which the logocentric system depends is displaced in such a way that it comes to occupy another position. In an interview, Derrida explained the process:

We must proceed using a double gesture, . . . a double writing, that is, a writing that is in and of itself multiple, what I called in *"La double séance," a double science.* On the one hand, we must traverse a phase of *overturning.* [. . .] To deconstruct [an] opposition, first of all, is to overturn the hierarchy at a given moment. [. . .]

That being said—and on the other hand—to remain in this phase is still to operate on the terrain of and from within the deconstructed system. By means of this double, and precisely stratified, dislodged and dislodging, writing, we must also mark the interval between inversion . . . and the irruptive emergence of a new "concept," a concept that can no longer be, and never could be, included in the previous regime.[. . .]This holds first of all for a new concept of writing, which *simultaneously* provokes the overturning of the hierarchy speech/writing, and the entire system attached to it, *and* releases the dissonance of writing within speech, thereby disorganizing the entire inherited order and invading the entire field. . . . [24]

This process leads Derrida, in the further course of his grammatological engagement, to develop his ideas in the framework of the "inherited order" that is impossible to abandon; however, his thinking can only be described as a series of paradoxes—as "non-" or "un-concepts": the "archetrace," "the supplement of (at) the origin," *différance.*

Derrida calls the signifier (whether letter or phonological sign) an "instituted trace." Insofar as what it signifies only follows in its wake, it is a trace of nothing—or, more precisely, the "original" trace preceding *what* it is a trace *of.* The signifier supplements something (the absence of a signified or an object) that, at the same time, is only given to consciousness through the signifier. Thus, it is an "original" supplement, for an "origin" conceived in this way can no longer be thought of as a fulfilled presence or, in Aristotelian terms, as a "first cause." What is secondary comes first; or, alternately, what seems to be primary (the origin, the *Ursache*) represents a belated projection—a retrofiction. Another term for the original trace of the signifier is *différance,* the inaudible neographism Derrida employs to bundle and collect different aspects of his thinking, which we will now explore in fuller detail.

The word or concept of *différance* (although, strictly speaking, what Derrida thereby designates is neither one nor the other) first occurs in *Speech and Phenomena.* He develops the notion at greater length in *Grammatology,* but the most elaborate exposition occurs in the essay "*Différance*" in *Margins of Philosophy*—a text that was originally a lecture. The difference between oral delivery and written work is significant insofar as Derrida discusses something that one cannot hear, but only read—the orthographic deviation between the normal French way of writing *différence* (with an *e*) and *différance* (with an *a*). This inaudible deviation illustrates that, strictly speaking, phonographic writing represents an impossibility: the two words are not written in the same way, yet their pronunciation is identical (that is, they are homophonic yet allographic). The letters do not represent sounds in an unequivocal manner. Derrida's lecture addresses a matter one cannot hear—something that is not evident in the spoken word, in the voice. But more is at stake than just a game of paradox.

Like the Latin *differre*, from which it derives, the French verb *différer* has two senses. On the one hand, it means *to deviate, vary, differ*; on the other hand—with reference to time—it signifies *to delay, postpone*. In French, the noun *différence* (with an *e*) designates only *difference, deviation*, or *variation*, whereas the words for delay or postponement are *le délai* or *la temporisation*. *Différence* (with an *e*) also does not include *differences* in the sense of conflict or disagreement ("they have some differences"); to express this idea, French has the word *le différend*, a formation tied to the present participle and the gerund. "The word differance (with an *a*)," Derrida writes, "is to compensate—economically—[for this] loss of meaning."[25] Since the *a* in *différance* derives immediately from the present participle of *différer* (*différant*), *différance* can connote deviation both in the sense of "distinction" and in the sense of "temporal delay." Moreover, because of the homophony that exists between *différend* and *différant*, the word also connotes conflict in the sense of "having differences." The term "can refer simultaneously to the entire configuration of its meanings. It is immediately and irreducibly polysemic, which will not be indifferent to the economy of my discourse here."[26]

Even more importantly: whereas *différence* (with an *e*) conventionally designates the static condition of a given distinction (the classical conception of variation between "positive elements"), the ending *-ance* (instead of *-ence*) displaces, on account of its proximity to continuous verbal aspect, the accent onto the *movement* or the *happening* of difference through delays over time—a phenomenon without a subject or agent, Derrida is quick to add.

In a conceptuality adhering to classical strictures, "*différance*" would be said to designate a constitutive, productive, and originary causality, the process of scission and division which would produce or constitute different things or differences.[27]

What is written *différance*, then, will be the playing movement that "produces"—by means of something that is not simply an activity—these differences, these effects of difference. This does not mean that the *différance* that produces differences is somehow before them, in a simple and unmodified—in-different—present.

Différance is the non-full, non-simple, structured and differentiating origin of differences.[28]

Différance (with an *a*) consists of a process of *differentiation* that is "spatializing" and "temporalizing" at once; it must always already have been in effect for discrete differences between "positive elements" to be identifiable at all. (If Derrida avoids the noun "differentiation," he does so because this word—which occurs in discourse about "social" or "biological" differentiation—evokes the idea of a substance that, whatever form it has assumed, is already given and differentiates itself afterward; *différance*, on the other hand, precedes all that is positively given and, indeed, makes positive "data" possible in the first place.)

What use, then, does such a "word" or "concept" offer? In fact, *différance* is not a word or a concept at all, because it marks the very precondition of conceptual thinking, of thought in distinct terms, and the possibility of speaking in an articulated manner. In the first place, Derrida employs the term to take up, once again, Saussure's principle of language as a field of unconscious differentiation. Also in the essay *"Différance,"* the "problematic of the sign" provides the first test case of the concept. Secondly, Derrida uses the neographism to *displace* Saussure's ideas in a way similar to the way he inverts the conventional understanding of writing. Thereby, he radicalizes what Saussure has begun and draws implications unforeseen by his predecessor.

As Derrida also stresses in *Grammatology*, the classical conception of the sign, with its distinction between signifier and signified (whatever form[s] the distinction assumes), itself belongs to the history of metaphysics. The line of separation between signifier and signified merges with the distinction between the sensible (i.e., the signifier—sound or letter) and the intelligible (the signified—concept, representation, [mental] image, meaning, *logos*); therefore, it remains linked with the model of language as representation. According to the classical logic of language, the fact that the sign re-presents implies that it makes something absent present (again), be it a "meaning" or an "object":

When we cannot grasp or show the thing, state the present, the being-present, when the present cannot be presented, we signify, we go through the detour of the sign. We take or give signs. We signal. The sign, in this sense, is deferred presence. Whether we are concerned with the verbal or the written sign, with the monetary sign, or with electoral delegation and political representation, the circulation of signs defers the moment in which we can encounter the thing itself, make it ours, consume or expend it, touch it, see it, intuit its presence.[29]

However, this *classical* thinking of the sign as an instance of place-holding-that-defers remains marked by the ideal that what is re-presented should become present again—a matter adequate to itself, which, now, is to be reproduced. It

presupposes that the sign, which defers presence, is conceivable only on the *basis* of the presence that it defers and *moving toward* the deferred presence that it aims to reappropriate. According to this classical semiology, the substitution of the sign for the thing itself is both *secondary* and *provisional*: secondary due to an original and lost presence from which the sign thus derives; provisional as it concerns this final and missing presence toward which the sign in this sense is a movement of mediation.[30]

Opposing this model of the sign as a placeholder mediating between two presences, the dynamic field of *différance* is constituted by a delay that is "original" and resistant to dialectical sublation. Neither in the past nor in the future will the presence of the "thing itself" ever be realized.

It is the *movement* of meaning itself (as the differential articulation of a chain of signifiers) that prevents a *single* meaning from ever coming to rest as something that can be appropriated outside the play of differences. There is no signified that, eluding dynamic tension between differences, might qualify as transcendental:

An interval must separate the present from what it is not in order for the present to be itself, but this interval that constitutes it as present must, by the same token, divide the present in and of itself, thereby also dividing, along with the present, everything that is thought on the basis of the present, that is, in our metaphysical language, every being, and singularly substance or the subject.[31]

The fact that the signified "is originarily and essentially . . . [a] trace [and] *always already in the position of the signifier*"[32] annuls the distinction between signifier and signified as a simple distinction between two substances (i.e., acoustic image and mental representation). *Différance* cannot be apprehended within the classical conception of the sign.

2.3 Some Consequences (Metaphor and Concept, Literature and Philosophy)

It follows from the foregoing that a certain logocentric concept of the sign and the "metaphysics of presence" belong together. One cannot address the first without, at the same time, questioning the second. Therefore, the conception of the sign offered by deconstruction holds a number of consequences. In terms of textual interpretation, it means that reading can no longer be understood as commentary that doubles its object. Reading does not involve recovering the original intention of an author as something that, preceding the play of differences, stands independent of it: "It seems to us in principle impossible to separate, through interpretation or commentary, the signified [that is, what was originally intended by the author—S.L.] from the signifier, and thus to destroy writing by the writing that is yet reading."[33]

If, all the same, commentary has a place in deconstruction, this is not because it might yet represent—or guarantee—the meaning of a text. Rather, it owes its importance to the fact that it creates a (historically determined) context within which to situate the act of interpretation. For the same reason, reading "cannot legitimately transgress the text toward something other than it, toward a referent (a reality that is metaphysical, historical, psychobiographical, etc.), or toward a signified outside the text whose content could take place, could have taken place outside of language, that is to say . . . outside of writing in general. [. . .] *There is nothing outside of the text*."[34]

Time and again, statements like this have led critics to view deconstruction as "omnilingualism" or "pantextualism." However, in this statement and others like it, it is not a matter of denying reality but of methodological rigor. *Readings* must stay within the text because they have no access to an extratextual signified (and this also means that one sometimes has *to read oneself*, because the signified of one's "own" text does not simply stand ready-at-hand either). Readings must be content to address signifiers—the data that is actually available for consultation and can be *read*. One must attend to signifiers and their distribution in a text—their constellation, repetitions, contradictions, and so on.

This is not a passive activity, but rather involves "a signifying structure that critical reading should *produce*."[35] Reading does so not by doubling the text through paraphrases (which generate something different from what stands written, anyway), but by establishing its own text. This "other" text remains anchored in the "primary" text, for it follows certain lines within it, marks determinate constellations of signifiers, and stresses a particular structure (and not others). For such a reading, the Archimedean point from which the totality of meaning within a text or a work of art is disclosed no longer exists—just as the (putative) intentions of the author do not furnish a definitive point of orientation. This is the case whether the reading involves a literary or a philosophical (theoretical) text. Just as the logocentric concept of the sign becomes problematic, so too do distinctions between logic and rhetoric, between concept and metaphor, and, more generally, between "literal" or "authentic" and "inauthentic" statements; as a result, the generic differences between philosophy (or theory) and literature also become blurred.

The canonical definition of metaphor (which means "transference" or, more literally, "carrying over") as a form of inauthentic communication derives, once again, from Aristotle: "Metaphor is the application to one thing of a name belonging to another thing; the transference may be from one species to another, or it may be a matter of analogy."[36] Such a broad definition corresponds, more or less, to the operative concept of figural language today, and, therefore, it is not limited to metaphor in particular (in contrast, say, to metonymy, synecdoche, or irony). Utterances employing tropes are deemed "inauthentic" in general. Such an understanding of metaphor is only possible within the theory of language-as-representation that we discussed above: it presumes that there is exactly one signified and one referent for every word.

Even more explicitly than Aristotle, the rhetorical tradition that followed him developed the doctrine of the *verbum proprium*—the "proper" or "authentic" word. Here, the meaning of a term is identified with the object it designates, and to which the word is supposed to stick, so to speak, as if it were a label. A metaphor is created when labels are exchanged—as when, for example, instead of saying "old age," one speaks of the "evening of life," or calls a camel a "ship of the desert." In this view, metaphor represents an act of expropriation and substitution—"sticker fraud," as it were.

It is no wonder, then, that philosophical tradition has regarded figures of speech with the same suspicion it has shown writing, and tried to restrict their use as much as possible. Poets may be permitted to avail themselves of metaphors as an "ornament of speech" (Quintilian), but for this same reason, what they say never seems free of elements of deception and ruse. Philosophers and scientists, on the other hand, are supposed to employ the "right words" and to use literal expressions instead of metaphors. According to this reasoning, a line of demarcation separates aesthetic *seeming* and true *being*, just as a boundary exists between metaphorical comparison and the conceptual definition of "objects." Only where no proper expression exists—as when something entirely new is referred to, which has no name as yet—is metaphor permitted as a step toward a proper designation in conceptual language.

The standard critique of metaphor extending well into the twentieth century relies upon the Aristotelian-rhetorical model of explanation. According to this line of reasoning, metaphors do not offer authentic designations; they are dis-placed, incapable of truth, and—because they are marked by ambiguity—obstacles to knowledge and insight. In the name of a rational understanding of language, metaphor has been rejected as a superfluous matter. When the theory of language as representation falls, however, the classical understanding of metaphor does, too. If language is defined as a system of *values*—in which the meaning of a sign can only be determined through its differential opposition to other signs—one can no longer distinguish categorically between the literal and figural meanings of words (or between denotation and connotation). It belongs to the *value* of the word "evening" that, in certain contexts, it can also signify "old age." The unavoidable polysemy (plurality of meanings) of signs characterizes not just metaphor, but the concept, as well. As Nietzsche already observed, every concept is the remainder of a (dead) metaphor. (The same is also true of the concept of "concept" itself, which exists thanks to transferring the concrete gesture of touching—*con-cipere*, in Latin—into the realm of the intelligible. And this also applies to the notion of metaphor, which is itself a metaphor.)

Not only is our everyday language full of metaphors—philosophical texts are, as well. Catachreses like "orange" or "table-leg" and figures of speech such as "my heart is breaking" or "hitting the nail on the head" provide examples from everyday language. To take an instance from philosophy, Plato relies on figural language when he calls the art of conversation "maieutics" (which means midwifery) because it helps to deliver truths that are supposed lie ready in the innate reason of every human being. To employ another philosophical turn of phrase, dialectical exchange "brings truth to light." This is a metaphor, too (like "the light of reason" itself), but one that, paradoxically, dismisses metaphor into the twilight of deception and the irrational. The use of figural language, then, offers no binding or absolute criterion for distinguishing literature and philosophy. The "inauthentic speech" excluded from the province of theory lodges at the heart of theory as its innermost possibility. Even philosophical texts owe their possibility to the play of signifiers which, at the same time, they try to govern, restrict, and neutralize. Clearly, the adventures of figural language resemble those of writing, which also returns where it is least expected.

Derrida devoted two essays to the subject: "White Mythology: Metaphor in the Text of Philosophy" (1971) and "The Retrait of Metaphor" (1987). Both these texts emphasize that the definition—and thereby the control and neutralization—of metaphor is a philosophical project. Philosophical discourse generates its other within itself even as it attempts to exclude it:

All the onomatism which dominates the theory of metaphor, and the entire Aristotelian doctrine of simple names (*Poetics*, 1457a) is elaborated in order to assure harbors of truth and propriety. [. . .] The necessity of examining the history and system of the value of "properness" has become apparent to us. An immense task. . . .[37]

The task is "immense" because it is not limited to deconstructing metaphors, or, as the case may be, undoing the opposition between concept and metaphor. Rather, it extends from the theory of signs into politics and ethics (cf. below). The structure Derrida develops apropos of metaphor— that is, the idea of an *originary tropical supplementarity* (first of language and then of desire)—also applies to other domains. What this means can perhaps be best illustrated with the example of metaphor itself.

In ancient Greek, *metaphorein* signifies "to take/carry somewhere else." In modern Greece, means of public transportation are actually called *metaphora*, because they take people from one location to another. In like fashion, metaphor carries a "simple name" somewhere else, removes it from its proper place, and, in the process, transforms it into an inauthentic designation. Thus, the concept of metaphor is itself a metaphor in that it transfers the seemingly simple activity of carrying-something-over from point A to point B into language. Philosophical discourse therefore employs metaphor to grasp the metaphorical—and to exclude it from itself. However, the metaphor of metaphor does not, in fact, replace a "simple name," for there is no other name for metaphor. The formation of the concept itself is metaphorical at its origin—that is, the metaphor of metaphor supplements or replaces a "simple name" that does not exist. Metaphor is the *original supplement.*

The object of definition (metaphor) is supposed to be excluded from what defines it (i.e., philosophical discourse), *yet at the same time, and as a genuinely philosophical metaphor, it remains included in the discourse that tries to banish it.* Likewise, philosophical discourse remains included in metaphor: it cannot escape metaphor, because even its way of taking distance from metaphor depends on metaphor. When the purity of philosophical discourse (as the asylum of truth and "simple names") is threatened, however, so is the identity of metaphor. If concepts are *already* metaphors, and metaphors are *still* concepts, then the distinction between concept and metaphor loses its ontological value. This is why it would be mistaken to refer to the concept of writing developed in *Grammatology* as metaphorical (inauthentic, a matter of transference, etc.). Metaphor "withdraws from the worldwide scene, and does so at the moment of its most invasive extension, at the instant it overflows every limit."[38] In the same sense, one reads in *Dissemination* that, "[when] everything becomes metaphorical, there is no longer any literal meaning and, hence, no longer any metaphor either."[39]

Statements like the preceding have contributed, time and again, to claims that Derrida pursues the anarchic "liquidation" and "leveling of distinctions" between literature and philosophy (or, as the case may be, between literature and science). For example, Jürgen Habermas has opined that deconstruction leads to "the borders between literal and metaphorical meaning, between logic and rhetoric, and between serious and fictional speech [being] washed away in the flow of a universal textual occurrence."[40] As opposed to the project he attributes to Derrida, Habermas calls for holding firm to the concept of rational self-consciousness and the project of Enlightenment. However, such allegations overlook the fact that Derrida in no way advocates deploying metaphor against concept, rhetoric against logic, or literature against philosophy and science. Rather, he shifts interest away from what literature and philosophy supposedly *are*, toward the ways that, in the course of Western history, they have distanced themselves from each other (and still do so). It is a matter of "[exploding] the reassuring opposition of the metaphoric and the proper, the opposition in which the one and the other have never done anything but reflect and refer to each other in their radiance."[41] When *interpreting*, one must still consider whether a text considers itself to be "literature" or "philosophy." Moreover, both literature and philosophy are institutionalized discourses that obey different rules of production. "Even if there is never a pure signified," we read in *Grammatology*, "there are different relationships as to that which, from the signifier, *is presented* as the irreducible stratum of the signified."[42] Therefore, a philosophical or theoretical text—as opposed to a literary one—"includes, precisely as its philosophical specificity, the project of effacing itself in the face of the signified content which it transports and in general teaches. Reading should be aware of this project, even if, in the last analysis, it intends to expose the project's failure."[43]

Derrida addresses the matter of literature as an institution above all in "The Law of Genre" (1980) and "Before the Law" (1980), essays that perform readings of *Madness of the Day*, by Maurice Blanchot, and Franz Kafka's parable of the doorkeeper from *The Trial*, respectively. However, the relationship between literature and philosophy already provides a theme in *Grammatology*, apropos of Rousseau, to whom the second part of the book is devoted.

2.4 The Desire for Presence and the Chain of Supplements (Rousseau)

The second half of *Grammatology* introduces Rousseau in a double capacity. In the first place, Rousseau provides a "case study" or an "example" to illustrate the "theoretical foundation" developed in the first part of the book. Secondly, as one who grapples with the specificity of writing, Rousseau bears witness to the double nature of writing in literary and philosophical praxis:

[Rousseau] produced a philosophical literature . . . and chose to live by literary writing; by a writing which would not be exhausted by the message—philosophical or otherwise—which it could, so to speak, deliver. And what Rousseau has said, as a philosopher . . . of writing in general, cannot be separated from the system of his own writing.[44]

Derrida's reading of Rousseau follows a key motif in Rousseau's texts: the figure of the supplement. By identifying a "signifying structure" within Rousseau's text, this reading shows at the same time the operative principles of its method.

"Languages are made to be spoken," Rousseau states in a classical manner; "writing only serves as a supplement to speech. . . . Speech represents thought by conventional signs, and writing represents the same with regard to speech. Thus the art of writing is nothing but a mediated representation of thought."[45] If, despite all this, Rousseau *writes*, he does so because, paradoxically, he cannot make himself understood in spoken communication. Others misunderstand him constantly and do not esteem him rightly: "I would enjoy society as much as the next man, if I were not certain to show myself there not only to my disadvantage, but as quite different from what I am. The decision that I took to write and to hide myself away was precisely the right one for me. Had I been more visible, no one would ever have known what I was worth, would not even have suspected it. . . . "[46] What brings Rousseau to writing, then, is his experience of speech that fails to perform what it promises. Oral communication is not how or what it *should* be—namely, the direct and immediate expression of interiority, the transparent outward show of what lies within. Rousseau's writing follows upon his wish to recreate the immediacy from which speech has been torn: "The first movement of this desire is formulated as a theory of language. The other governs the experience of the writer."[47] Both aspects of this desire seek to expunge supplements and to restore the simplicity of self-sufficient nature. Either way, the aim runs up against an original and unavoidable supplementarity that blocks "nature" and the "thing itself." Derrida follows the "chain of supplements" through Rousseau's text. First, Rousseau notes that childhood provides the first manifestation of a lack calling for remedy and assistance. Since children are, by nature, insufficient to themselves, one must "help them and supply what they lack, in intelligence or in strength, whenever the need is of the body."[48] Also human nature on the whole, however, is too weak to be self-sufficient: it needs culture to supplement its inadequacies and assure the survival of mankind. Thus, human beings invent tools where their inborn powers fail, and they invent language because they need to communicate with each other. (*Nota bene*: deficiency within nature itself necessitates these inventions!)

With language, however, begin the sufferings of memory and imagination, which are already supplements to replace a simple presence that is now gone. In Rousseau's case, what has to be replaced involves the presence of his mother, who died at his birth. He found a *replacement* for her in Madame de Warens, thirteen years his senior, whom he called *Maman* and whose "image" he "ceaselessly wooed in his fantasy." *Instead of her*, Rousseau kisses the bed where she has lain, the floor on which she has walked, and the objects she has touched. . . . Later, he replaces Maman with his wife Thérèse: "I needed, in short, a successor to Maman. [. . .] In Thérèse I discovered the substitute I needed."[49] In this context, another supplement is significant—and not just for Rousseau, but also for Derrida's reading of Rousseau: masturbation as substitute for intercourse. "I had learned to use that dangerous supplement which defrauds nature and saves young men of my temperament from many disorders, but at the expense of their health, their strength, and sometimes their life itself,"[50] he writes in the *Confessions*. In Book IV of *Émile*, one reads of onanism: "Once he knows this dangerous supplement, he is lost."[51]

If Derrida declares that this particular supplement possesses "paradigmatic value," he does so because autoeroticism and auto-affection overlap in the act of masturbation:

Sexual auto-affection, that is auto-affection in general, neither begins nor ends with what one thinks can be circumscribed by the name of masturbation. The supplement has not only the power of *procuring* an absent presence through its image; procuring it for us through the proxy of the sign, it holds it at a distance and masters it. For this presence is at the same time desired and feared.[52]

Rousseau: "This vice, so congenial to shame and timidity is, in addition, very attractive to those of a lively imagination, for it places at their disposal, as it were, the whole of the other sex, and makes any lovely woman that tempts them serve their desires without needing to obtain her consent.[53] Sexual auto-affection (which is to say, auto-affection in general) combines the gesture of domination with desire. Both are mediated by (mental) images—signs—which make the "thing itself" present *and*, at the same time, hold it at a distance, that is to say, *supplement* it. Therefore, autoeroticism illustrates the structure of supplementarity as such.

The supplement alternates between the *complement* of a thing and its *substitute*. On the one hand, "it is a surplus, a plenitude enriching another plenitude, the *fullest measure* of presence."[54] On the other hand, it tends to erase the "thing itself" and take its place. This is why, according to Rousseau, it is "dangerous"—a state of affairs equally true of masturbation and writing. Derrida turns this logic upside down and shows how, in fact, auto-affection and autoeroticism provide the *precondition* for allo-affection and desire for the other:

Within the general structure of auto-affection, within the giving-oneself-a-presence or a pleasure, the operation of touching-touched receives the other within the narrow gulf that separates doing from suffering. And the outside, the exposed surface of the body, signifies and marks forever the division that shapes auto-affection.

Auto-affection is a universal structure of experience. [. . .] And only a being capable of symbolizing, that is to say of auto-affecting, may let itself be affected by the other in general. Auto-affection is the condition of an experience in general.[55]

This also means that the supplement, the condition of supplementarity, provides the prerequisite for experience of the "thing itself"—that immediacy is predicated on mediation, presence on absence. Opposing terms come together in a state of mutual interdependence in the sign. Desire (for presence, for the Other, for the "thing itself") can only come about because—and insofar as—the object one seeks is simultaneously "there" *and* "not there": the sign makes it appear, yet holds it at a remove, too. Only a being that is capable of symbolism (which is to say, able to affect itself with an absent presence) can desire. Desire can only occur where reality is missing. Indeed, if a true convergence with what is really real were to occur, this would mean not only the death of desire, but also the death of consciousness. In different—and more drastic—terms: if intercourse (which Rousseau feared even more than masturbation) were not *always also* auto-affection (i.e., autoeroticism), it would not exist at all.

A relation to the other presupposes separation from the other:

> The enjoyment of the *thing itself* is thus undermined, in its act and in its essence, by frustration. One cannot therefore say that it has an essence or an act. . . . Something promises itself as it escapes, gives itself as it moves away [from enjoyment—S.L.], and strictly speaking it cannot even be called presence. Such is the constraint of the supplement. . . .[56]

The reading of Rousseau in the second part of *Grammatology*, then, also provides something that Derrida does not name explicitly: it illustrates not just the theory of the sign developed in the book's first part by way of example, but adds, as a supplement, a theory of desire. Both theories have the same structure: the "chain of supplements" consists of a chain of signifiers, and vice-versa. Desire, like the "simple name" of Aristotelian philosophy, does not have a fixed place, a natural location. The metaphors that constitute it stand in for authentic expression. Maman replaces the mother (i.e., nature), Thérèse replaces Maman, and masturbation takes the place of intercourse with either party. This is only possible because "the system of supplementarity [of language—S.L.] in general [was] already open in its possibility" and because "the play of substitutions [was] already operative for a long time": "*in a certain way Thérèse herself [was] already a supplement.* As Maman was already the supplement of an unknown mother, and as the 'true mother' herself, at whom the known 'psychoanalyses' of the case of Jean-Jacques Rousseau stop, was also in a certain way a supplement, from the first trace, and even if she had not 'truly' died in giving birth. Here is the chain of supplements."[57]

To be sure, Derrida is not interested simply in the personal pathology of Rousseau (the point where psychoanalytic interpretations of his "case" stop). Rather, he takes up Rousseau because the latter, more visibly than others, stood at the threshold of modernity, even if he was unaware of this fact and articulated *the structure of the signifier and the structure of desire itself.* He occupied a position where it was possible to do so thanks to a *literary* mode of writing, which set out to say *everything*—even at the expense of coherence. In the process, he crafted a text that conflicts with his own theoretical convictions:

Rousseau condemns writing as destruction of presence and as disease of speech. He rehabilitates it to the extent that it promises the reappropriation of that of which speech allowed itself to be dispossessed. But by what, if not already a writing older than speech and already installed in that place?[58]

Rousseau calls this location his "heart." Today, one would speak of his "unconscious." The first lines of the *Confessions* read:

> I am resolved on an undertaking that has no model and will have no imitator. I want to show my fellow-men a man in all the truth of nature; and this man is to be myself.
>
> Myself alone. I read in my heart and I know men. I am not made like any that I have seen. [. . .] As to whether nature did well or ill to break the mould in which I was cast, that is something no one can judge until after they have read me.[59]

Modern literature begins with words like these. Its paradigm is auto-biography. "To write means: to read oneself," Max Frisch observed in a celebrated dictum. "One is what one is. One uses one's pen like the needle of a seismograph: we do not so much write as get written. To write means: to read oneself."[60] But this also means that one *is bound to* read oneself, for the I-that-writes is not transparent; it does not dispose, in sovereign fashion, over the thoughts it first has and then "expresses." If, as Derrida affirms, "the irreducibility of writing and . . . the subversion of logocentrism are announced better than elsewhere . . . in a certain sector and a certain determined form of 'literary' practice,"[61] this is the case because, in modern literature, the act of writing is fused with the act of self-reading.

Therefore, in the modern world, one can call "literary" those practices of writing that, from the inception, can be reduced neither to the spoken word nor to meaning "contained" by speech. If, then—as Derrida himself does, too—we put the word "literary" in quotation marks, it serves to highlight the fact that we are not concerned with defining a supra-historical or substantial "essence" of literature. Instead, "literature" names a relatively recent institution, which developed around 1800 and, since then, has subordinated writing to certain juridical, political, and aesthetic conditions of production. The institution includes certain notions of authorship, work, and intellectual property (which stand firm, still today, in copyright law) that are in line with the metaphysical concept of the subject as *auctor* (the creator and master of signifying matter). It also means that this institution of fiction . . . gives *in principle* the power to say everything, to break free of the rules, to displace them. . . . Here we should ask juridical and political questions. The institution of literature in the West, in its relatively modern form, is linked to an authorization to say everything, and doubtless too to the coming about of the modern idea of democracy. Not that it depends on a democracy in place, but it seems inseparable to me from what calls forth a democracy, in the most open (and doubtless itself to come) sense of democracy.[62]

If only through so-called "artistic freedom"—which represents a fundamental right—literature can indeed be distinguished from philosophy and science. On the one hand, modern democracies also embrace the "freedom of science," with the same guarantees (chiefly, to be free of political instrumentalization); however, the latter is still bound to the obligations of truth and a certain method. What is allowed in fiction (say, in a novel) becomes an error—or a lie—in a scientific treatise.

The freedom to say anything and everything, along with a new model of self-presence: the self-presence of the subject in conscience and feeling; this freedom privileges, one might say, a new kind of "literary" experience of the primacy of writing which is no longer logocentric. In this sense, Derrida affirms that deconstruction means "coming to terms with literature"—which does not mean claiming that philosophy and literature are indistinguishable. Philosophy has always attempted to exclude literature: the opposition between *mythos* (literally, "narrative," "invented story") and *logos* is just as central to its self-definition as is the distinction between metaphor and concept. If Derrida seeks to tarry at the "border" or at the "margins" of philosophical discourse, he does so in order to shake the "system of fundamental constraints, conceptual oppositions outside of which philosophy becomes impracticable"[63]—to bring it into movement from within and from without, simultaneously. Literature provides one such margin of philosophical discourse; psychoanalysis provides another. Unlike psychoanalysis, however, literary texts (barring those of Rousseau, perhaps) do not offer an object for *deconstructive* readings in the proper sense. Instead, Derrida seeks to deconstruct philosophical discourse from the standpoint of literature and the different position it assigns to writing; in the process, philosophy undergoes a transformation. Once again, Nietzsche and Heidegger may be seen as forerunners or models, for these philosophers practiced forms of writing that, to a significant degree, employed "literary" forms, as they have been understood traditionally (metaphors, parables, irony, etc.). Heidegger already stressed that the proximity of poetry and thought (*Dichten und Denken*) offered a way to gain an "experience of language."

Derrida also wrote texts that, by the conventions of philosophical reasoning, are "literary" in nature—above all *Envois*, the first part of *The Post Card* (1980), which consists of fictitious missives to a person whose identity is never revealed. Time and again, these "postcards"—which are, by turns, written in an associative manner and then in a way that follows a strict structure of argumentation—refer to a picture representing Plato and Socrates; here, the one stands behind the other and makes a pointing gesture with his finger. In the almost maniacally repeated descriptions of the scene (which a facsimile print in the appendix reproduces), the relationship between Socrates and Plato achieves an erotic coloration. Then, the voice of Freud appears in the exchange. In this way, a question becomes more and more pronounced: to whom is Derrida writing—and who is (really) writing? The freedom of literature is enacted: the power to raise—and leave open—the question of who it is that speaks, and to let the instances of discourse proliferate. . . . In *The Post Card*—which is concerned with the possibilities and dead-ends of communication (and contains an extensive critique of Lacan)—the inaugural section gives dramatic form to the issues that provide the central concern of the rest of the volume.

Deconstruction, then, touches not only on the self-understanding, but also on the affective bases of Western culture. When Derrida writes that the "return of writing" also signifies the loss of presence as the "matrix of Being," he has chosen his words carefully. As when he employs psychoanalytic vocabulary, Derrida hereby indicates that deconstruction also implies an "insult to human self-love" (Freud), for metaphysics does not consist of a system of moral values alone, but also of affective investments. It implies not just concepts and value-oppositions, but also desire: desire for presence (of meaning, or of the "thing itself), desire for truth and insight, and desire for identity, "authenticity," belonging, autonomy, and dominion. In this sense, Derrida observes, our everyday language is "neither harmless nor neutral. It *is* the language of Western metaphysics and carries with it an array of assumptions"; these assumptions are also operative even if one knows nothing about them—even if one is not a philosopher or an academic and has never read a word of Plato, Hegel, Heidegger, or Derrida himself.

If (if!) the epoch of metaphysics is nearing an end today, then more is at stake than just a theory of signs or a philosophical or hermeneutic ideal. The matter concerns the variable conditions of possibility for the ways we think and live, which remain largely unarticulated as yet. In a sense, then, deconstruction represents a kind of "anamnesis"—in the double sense of "re-collection," on the one hand, and "medical history," on the other. This is because the history of Western metaphysics represents the sum-total of the psychic, physical, and political exercise of violence in the name of the highest values, which culminated in twentieth-century totalitarian regimes. Ultimately, it is not terribly important whether the wars of the Western world were conducted in the name of God, Kaiser, nation, or race. In each case, all ideological systems rest upon *centered structures* that are grouped around a *privileged term*. As Derrida observes, this term functions as a "transcendental signified," which refers the structure "to a point of presence"[64]—a presence that is to be protected, defended, and reconstituted, which provides both the origin and the end goal of the system in question. The philosophical and the political systems of the West all have *the same structure*: "It could be shown that all the names related to fundamentals, to principles, or to the center have always designated an invariable presence."[65]

Third Approach: There Are "Undeconstructibles" (Are There?)

A new categorical imperative has been imposed by Hitler upon unfree mankind: to arrange their thoughts and actions so that Auschwitz will not repeat itself, so that nothing similar will happen. When we want to find reasons for it, this imperative is as refractory as the given one of Kant was once upon a time. Dealing discursively with it would be an outrage, for the new imperative gives us a bodily sensation of the moral addendum.

—Theodor W. Adorno, *Negative Dialectics*

I can only describe my feeling by the metaphor, that, if a man could write a book on Ethics which really was a book on Ethics, this book would, with an explosion, destroy all the other books in the world.

—Ludwig Wittgenstein, "Lecture on Ethics"

3.1 Violence-Law-Justice

Beginning in the late 1980s, Derrida devoted himself more and more, and in an increasingly direct fashion, to political and ethical themes. The essay, "Force of Law: The Mystical Foundation of Authority" (1990), which first appeared in English, seems to mark a turning point, insofar as here, for the first time, the matter of what is "undeconstructible"—or, more precisely, the undeconstructibility of justice as a pendant to positive law—stands at issue. In the 1990s and early 2000s, the related topics of the gift, the Other, hospitality, and the event received Derrida's attention, especially in *Given Time: Counterfeit Money* (1991), *The Gift of Death* (1992), and *Of Hospitality* (1997). Besides these texts, which focus on the political ethics of responsibility in the broadest terms, Derrida published deconstructive works in the narrower sense, which explore, above all, the Western concept of the political and the idea of a coming democracy (*démocratie à venir*): *The Other Heading* (1991), *Specters of Marx* (1993), *Politics of Friendship* (1994), *Rogues* (2003), and *Philosophy in a Time of Terror* (2003).

"Force of Law" goes back to a lecture Derrida delivered at the Cardozo Law School in New York at a colloquium entitled *Deconstruction and the Possibility of Justice*. The occasion of the conference is significant insofar as it gave Derrida the opportunity to articulate deconstruction's goals and fundamental engagement, and to situate the position it occupied (or should occupy) not just in the production of knowledge, but also in the intellectual and political debates of the time. For this reason, the essay deserves our full attention.

Since its foundation in 1976, the Benjamin N. Cardozo School of Law has been a center of Critical Legal Studies, a progressive current of American legal theory. Activities there are distinguished, in particular, by an interest in European thinking—first, Critical Theory and subsequently poststructuralism (Foucault, Derrida, Lacan), insofar as they challenge the positivism and market liberalism that otherwise dominate American legal institutions. Its essential concerns remain the critique of the American system from within and the analysis of the relationships between social power and law.

Ever since the 1966 convocation of structuralists in Baltimore, Derrida had been no stranger to the United States. He taught regularly at Yale, Johns Hopkins, and, later, the University of California, Irvine. For the most part, however—and as occurred in Europe, too—the reception of deconstruction was restricted to literary studies, whereas academic philosophy and political theory either took no notice at all or met Derrida's project with attitudes ranging from rejection to outright hostility. (To the present day, this has not changed much.) The interest in deconstruction demonstrated by American legal studies seemed to offer a chance to overcome the situation, and the title of the conference—*Deconstruction and the Possibility of Justice*—indicated that it was perhaps time to confront prejudices against deconstruction and, possibly, discard them.

Counter to widespread opinion, Derrida submits, "what is currently called deconstruction [does] not correspond (though certain people have an interest in spreading this confusion) to a quasi-nihilistic abdication before the ethico-politico-juridical question of justice and before the opposition between the just and the unjust."[1] He then affirms that "a deconstructive interrogation that starts . . . by destabilizing, complicating, or bringing out the paradoxes of values like those of the proper and of property in all their registers, of the subject, and so of the responsible subject, of the subject of law (*droit*) and the subject of morality, of the juridical or moral person, of intentionality, etc., . . . such a deconstructive line of questioning is through and through a problematization of law and justice."[2] The field of law, laws, and justice (and therefore law schools, too) is the "proper place" for investigations of a deconstructive nature (if, in fact, such a thing as a "proper place" for deconstruction exists); at any rate, it is a more fitting location than departments of literary study, "where [deconstruction has] often been thought to belong."[3]

Derrida therefore greets the emergence of Critical Legal Studies as "among the most fertile and the most necessary" developments:

[It] respond[s], it seems to me, to the most radical programs of a deconstruction that would like, in order to be consistent with itself, not to remain enclosed in purely speculative, theoretical, academic discourse but rather . . . aspire to something more consequential, to *change* things and to intervene in an efficient and responsible though always, of course, very mediated way, not only in the profession but in what one calls the *cité*, the polis and more generally the world. . . . [I]n the sense of maximum intensification of a transformation in progress. . . .[4]

"[A] transformation in progress": on the one hand, these words can be understood in reference to changes in the production of knowledge, which, especially in the United States, were beginning to take an increasingly interdisciplinary direction. On the other hand, Derrida was speaking in 1989, when the Berlin Wall fell, the Soviet Union collapsed, and the Cold War ended. It was also the inception of a media revolution through the commercialization of computers and the emergence of the world wide web. These developments held massive consequences for the way geopolitical and cultural space was configured, and they put into question "the values of the proper and of property" (and still do): the "proper" definition of scholarly disciplines, of the nation-state and governmental sovereignty, of the identity of the West and local or regional communities. Suddenly, "deconstruction" no longer seemed to be just a philosophical project within the confines of academia, but something occurring on its own beyond academia, "out in the world."

If, against this backdrop, Derrida turned to the relationship between law and justice, he was also concerned with demonstrating the sociopolitical relevance of deconstruction. He begins by putting into question the standard opposition between law and violence, pointing out that each concrete, positive institution of law, every operative state legal system, has violence at its foundation and requires violence (on the part of both the government and the police) to assert and maintain itself. The English word "enforceability," Derrida observes, "reminds us that there is no such thing as law (*droit*) that doesn't imply *in itself, a priori, in the analytic structure of its concept*, the possibility of being 'enforced,' applied by force."[5] The possibility, in a given legal system, in any particular case, of distinguishing between legal and illegal, or legitimate and illegitimate, uses of force does not affect the core contamination of law and violence. On the one hand, such a distinction occurs only *after* the implementation of positive law; on the other, there is (therefore) no pre-existing order guaranteeing that legally and legitimately practiced violence is also just. The moment when law is instituted, whether through a revolutionary act or through the annexation of land, is *per definitionem* law-less (neither in keeping with law or against it); it occurs as a moment of political violence that precedes the distinction between right and wrong and, at the same time, founds this distinction.

The violent structure of the inaugural act remains inscribed within the law—this is the suspension of the law itself as *epoché* (bracketing of judgment), the impossibility of an absolute foundation, a blind spot, which Montaigne (and, after him, Pascal) had called the "mystical foundation of authority":

Laws remain in credit not because they are just, but because they are laws. That is the mystical foundation of their authority; they have no other. [. . .] Whoever obeys them because they are just, does not obey them for the reason he should.[6]

Following reason alone, nothing is intrinsically just; everything moves with the times. Custom is the whole of equity for the sole reason that it is accepted. That is the mystical basis of its authority. Whoever tries to trace this authority back to its origin, destroys it.[7]

Neither reason nor religion (revealed truth) nor justice provides the source of law—only violence and "custom." This is a specifically modern thought, which (in a certain way already for Montaigne and Pascal) founds the *deconstructibility* of law. It is "constructed on interpretable and transformable textual strata (and that is the history of law [*droit*], its possible and necessary transformation, sometimes its amelioration); . . . its ultimate foundation is by definition unfounded. The fact that law is deconstructible is not bad news, we may even see in this a stroke of luck for politics, for all historical progress."[8]

Now, Derrida contrasts law that can be deconstructed (criticized, discussed, and changed) with justice. Justice, he affirms, is *not deconstructible*. In a turn that seems breathtaking at first, Derrida equates this undeconstructible justice with deconstruction itself:

Justice in itself, if such a thing exists, outside or beyond law, is not deconstructible. No more than deconstruction itself, if such a thing exists. Deconstruction is justice. [. . .] Deconstruction takes place in the interval that separates the undeconstructibility of justice from the deconstructibility of *droit* (authority, legitimacy, and so on). It is possible as an experience of the impossible, there where, even if it does not exist (or does not yet exist, or never does exist), *there is* justice. Wherever one can replace, translate, determine the X of justice, one should say: deconstruction is possible, as impossible, to the extent (there) where *there is* (undeconstructible) X, thus to the extent (there) where *there is* (the undeconstructible).[9]

The conception of justice Derrida sets forth enables an initial understanding of this difficult passage. Thereby, he indirectly takes position in a debate that has governed political philosophy in America since the 1970s—a debate triggered by John Rawls's *A Theory of Justice*, which appeared in 1971. Rawls had defined justice as fairness. Following in Kant's footsteps, he laid out general principles for the just constitution of society:

A set of principles is required for choosing among the various social arrangements which determine [the] division of advantages and for underwriting an agreement on the proper distributive shares. These principles are the principles of social justice: they provide a way of assigning rights and duties in the basic institutions of society and they define the appropriate distribution of the benefits and burdens of social cooperation.[10]

For us the primary subject of justice is the basic structure of society, or . . . the way in which the major social institutions distribute fundamental rights and duties and determine the division of advantages. . . .[11]

An intensive debate on the question of justice spanned the last thirty years of the twentieth century. Critiques of the liberal egalitarianism advocated by Rawls and Ronald Dworkin came from radical-liberal authors such as Robert Nozick, Friedrich Hayek, and James Buchanan; from the perspective of communitarianism, which focuses on the welfare of society as a whole, critiques were also made by the likes of Charles Taylor, Michael Sandel, Alasdair MacIntyre, and Michael Walzer.

Despite differences in the way they understand the relationship between individual and community, egalitarians and communitarians share a conception of justice that may be defined, in a very broad sense, as *economic*, for the underlying concern involves the distribution (or redistribution) of material and immaterial goods (social justice, equal opportunity, equality before the law), removing disadvantages in access to social positions (compensatory justice), making good for damages inflicted (restorative justice), and retribution for wrongs committed (penal justice). One may argue, from case to case, about *what* distribution, reallocation, or punishment is right; however, it stands beyond dispute that what is appropriate in each instance is in principle measurable—and that this quantifiable standard of justice follows a general principle of reciprocity.

Against such a view, Derrida brings a fully different conception of justice into play—one that, at least in the claims it makes, does not permit economy, symmetry, measurement, or calculation:

Every time that something comes to pass or turns out well, every time that we placidly apply a good rule to a particular case, to a correctly subsumed example, according to a determinant judgment, we can be sure that law (*droit*) may find itself accounted for, but certainly not justice. Law is the element of calculation, and it is just that there be law, but justice is incalculable, it requires us to calculate with the incalculable.[12]

In contrast to law, Derrida's conception of justice does not entail subsumption, the effort to compare and balance out competing claims, or reciprocity. Instead, notwithstanding its universality, it is a matter of recognizing the absolute singularity of the individual.

Here, Derrida invokes Emmanuel Levinas, with whom he was joined in lifelong friendship and whose ethics of the Other he discussed on many occasions ("Violence and Metaphysics," "At This Very Moment in This Work Here I Am," *The Gift of Death, Adieu*). Since 1930, Levinas had played a key role in diffusing Husserl's phenomenology in France. Unlike Derrida, however, he understood himself to be a Jewish philosopher above all. At the center of his work stands the endeavor to affirm "ethics as a first philosophy"; like deconstruction, the project's goal is to overcome the tradition of ontology. According to the analysis set forward in "Violence and Metaphysics" (1964), Derrida's first significant discussion of Levinas, the latter does not "seek to propose laws or moral rules, does not seek to determine a morality, but rather the essence of the ethical relation in general."[13] Above all, this attempt occurs because of the failure of inherited forms of moral philosophy at Auschwitz. Levinas responds to such inadequacy with an ethics that no longer takes the subject and its moral faculty of judgment as a point of departure, but which is instead based on the unqualified claims of the Other, to whom the subject is beholden. Therefore, in Levinas's main works, *Totality and Infinity* (1961) and *Otherwise than Being: Or Beyond Essence* (1974), phenomenological analyses of face-to-face encounters with the Other stand at the center, underscoring the absolute asymmetry of this foundational relationship. Justice, for Levinas, lies here alone; indeed, it is only possible *as* this relationship to the Other, to whom the subject must answer. In "Force of Law," we read:

I would be tempted, up to a certain point, to compare the concept of justice—which I'm here trying to distinguish from law—to Levinas's, just because of this infinity and because of the heteronomic relation to others, to the faces of otherness that govern me, whose infinity I cannot thematize and whose hostage I remain. In *Totalité et Infini . . .*, Levinas writes: "the relation to others—that is to say, justice."[14]

Derrida also indicates that this conception of justice has its basis in what Levinas called "Jewish humanism," which approaches "the Hebrew equivalent of what we would perhaps translate as "sanctity."[15] The Hebrew word for "holy" (*kadosh*) has, as its root meaning, "particular" or "special," and it stands in opposition to "profane" ("worldly," "normal," "everyday").

To what extent, then, when understood *from a standpoint close to that of Levinas*, is justice undeconstructible? Is this undeconstructibility something "technical" in the sense that the method of deconstruction cannot address justice, inasmuch as it cannot be "applied"? Or are we facing a commandment, an ethical imperative: "Justice *should not*— it *may not*—be deconstructed"? The following passage suggests the latter:

No; what motivates deconstruction—the undeconstructible which, in this context, is given the name justice, as distinguished from law or right (*droit*)—does not take the form of a founding limit where a kind of radical doubt would be arrested, which it butts up against. It is an injunction which any construction or foundation would be inadequate to.[16]

Of the imperative of justice: "Be just!" it can only be said that *it is there* (or that it is *given*)—as a call, an exhortation, which issues from the Other to me, without my ever being able to be certain whether I have fulfilled it; indeed, I can never know whether I am able to fulfill it.

When Derrida affirms that this undeconstructible injunction brings deconstruction into motion, that it provides its decisive impulse or animating force, he subordinates his own work to an ethical imperative— an *X* (of justice), in whose name something like deconstruction occurs. Deconstruction, then, means attempting to do justice to things (be they persons, texts, or systems of thought)—taking them seriously in their singularity or idiomaticity, which cannot be subsumed. Thereby, it is also implied that deconstruction, the stripping-off or elimination of sedimentary structures of judgment and decision, provides the precondition for justice to take place; in this sense, when deconstruction occurs, it also "is" the event of justice.

Derrida's focus on indeconstructibility has led some to speak of an "ethical" or a "performative" turn in his thinking. This implies that Derrida left behind the critique of metaphysics in order to develop a postmetaphysical ethics. Whether one shares this assessment or, instead, sees continuity between earlier and later texts, depends, to a large extent, on the significance one accords to Derrida's relationship with Emmanuel Levinas and his ethics of the Other—that is, whether one reads Derrida "with Levinas" or "against" (or, indeed, "without") him.

However one responds to the question—a discussion of its nuances exceeds what an introductory work can offer—it is clear that Derrida's claim is highly charged. The performative gesture with which he simply *posits* justice and other values—the Other, the gift, hospitality—seems presumptuous, even if (or precisely because) he does not—and cannot— affirm a *fundamentum inconcussum* (a foundation beyond question) for deconstruction, comparable to the "I think" of philosophical tradition. Statements such as "justice is undeconstructible" and "deconstruction is justice" are bold, to say the least. One could also call them pathos-laden, for they strike a very fragile bridge over "the mystical ground of authority" (in this case, of Derrida's own academic and intellectual authority). This bridge is fragile not least because it employs the same form of judgment ("A is B") that Derrida elsewhere—and even in "Force of Law" itself—criticizes and dismisses as metaphysical. To be sure, Derrida is aware of this performative self-contradiction. If, all the same, he says (or writes) these sentences "without a safety net" (so to speak), his decision *offers matter for thought.* Above all, it means thinking about what remains implicit in "Force of Law," matters concerning the relationship between undecidability and decision.

In the first chapter of this study, we saw that the critique of metaphysics first unfolds as a critique of language and the form of judgment, insofar as it contains certain assumptions about being. In "Force of Law," Derrida directs his gaze at a particular and institutionalized form of judgment, namely judicial decision. The latter has certain points in common with general logical and grammatical forms of judgment, for every act of judgment *subsumes*—that is, it subordinates a phenomenon to a concept (or one concept to another). If I say, "The sky is blue," "This is a leaf," or "A camel is a mammal," then I am subsuming the sky under the sum of all blue things, "this thing here" under the category of leaves, and the camel under the class of animals that nurse their young. In law, subsumption involves applying a legal norm to a state of affairs in life (a "case"); it means subordinating specific circumstances to the general conditions constituting a norm. For example, Paragraph 211 of the German Penal Code declares: "He is a murderer who, out of the desire for blood [*aus Mordlust*], to satisfy a sexual urge, out of covetousness, or otherwise from base motives, in order to make another punishable act possible or to conceal [such an act], maliciously and by homicidal means, kills a human being." Whether or not someone falls under the classification of "murderer" (as opposed to "merely" having committed manslaughter, say) depends on whether the act of killing at issue demonstrates the qualities the murderer possesses according to legal statute. To determine if this is so, and to arrive at a fitting judgment, is the task of the judge.

But whether we are discussing murderers, leaves, or camels, subsumption is based on the comparability of a concrete, individual case and other instances: the concept of "murderer" applies to all murderers, the concept "leaf" is valid for all leaves, and so on, irrespective of the particular traits that *only occur in this particular* murder, leaf, or camel. Such comparability is not only implied in acts of judgment, but is already contained in the definition of the concepts themselves. In this sense, Nietzsche already wrote, apropos of "the formation of concepts":

Every word instantly becomes a concept precisely insofar as it is not supposed to serve as a reminder of the unique and entirely individual original experience to which it owes its origin; but rather, a word becomes a concept insofar as it simultaneously has to fit countless more or less similar cases—which means, purely and simply, cases which are never equal and thus altogether unequal. [. . .] We obtain the concept, as we do the form, by overlooking what is individual and actual; whereas nature is acquainted with no forms and no concepts, and likewise with no species, but only with an X which remains inaccessible and undefinable for us. For even our contrast between individual and species is something anthropomorphic and does not originate in the essence of things; although we should not presume to claim that this contrast does not correspond to the essence of things: that would of course be a dogmatic assertion and, as such, would be just as indemonstrable as its opposite.[17]

By equating what is "never equal" and "overlooking what is individual," the concept, *qua* concept, already misses the singularity of the individual case, the concrete phenomenon. This may be acceptable where leaves or camels are concerned, but in the event of murder or manslaughter, it is problematic. The legal system knows as much, of course, and tries to provide a corrective through general principles of law such as the notion of justice-in-the-individual-case [*Einzelfallgerechtigkeit*] (which grants a certain discretionary power to the judge—for example, in determining the extent of punishment) and the possibility of appeal (as a legal recourse against a sentence that has already been passed and is perceived as "unjust").

And so, already within the law itself, justice comes into play as a "higher" measure of the subsumption that occurs as a matter of course; it represents awareness of the relativity and fallibility (which exceeds the fallibility of the individual judge or individual judgment) that affect the law. Provisos built into the law itself may change, yet no provision exists for the basic and inevitable inadequacy of concepts and judgments concerning the "essence of things"—the always-singular and incomparable

X of an individual, concrete phenomenon. Derrida's concept of justice concerns *this* level, where correct or false subsumption no longer stands at issue, and it is not a matter of criticizing this or that judgment; it makes a fundamental claim that the form of judgment itself is inherently "unjust" (i.e., it does not involve the negation of a particular instance of judgment, but means the negation of the form of judgment itself). *No judgment of the Other is possible in which the form of judgment does not already mistake the Other in his singularity; in this sense, injustice is guaranteed.*

Of course, such a lofty conception of justice seems unsuited to the law; decisions must be reached. If, nevertheless, it comes into play—and, according to Derrida, it *must* come into play—this is only possible in aporetic form, as the experience of competing and contradictory demands on the process of legal decision:

1. In order for a decision to be both just and responsible, it must, "in its proper moment, if there is one, be both regulated and without regulation."[18] The judge may not judge arbitrarily, but must follow the law in his judgment, apply the prescriptions or rules of law to the individual case. At the same time, "each case is other, each decision is different and requires an absolutely unique interpretation, which no existing, coded rule can or ought to guarantee absolutely."[19] The judge must reach a decision as if, in each particular case, it were a matter of inventing the law and justifying it anew.

2. Only a decision (a judgment) can be just. A given decision (a given judgment), however, is, at the same time, necessarily also unjust, because it always encounters what is singular and there-fore undecidable. "The undecidable is not merely the oscillation or the tension between two decisions; it is the experience of that which, though heterogeneous, foreign to the order of the calcula-ble and the rule, is still obliged—it is of obligation that we must speak—to give itself up to the impossible decision, while taking account of law and rules."[20]

3. For a decision to be just, it must be reached by "the best knowl-edge." However, the knowledge that is required to arrive at a decision—because it is knowledge of a concrete case in its par-ticularity—is, in principle and always, incomplete, inconclusive.

> At the same time, justice "cannot wait"—a decision must be reached sooner or later. Even if it disposed of infinite knowledge, as something finite, it would still be the instance that closes the horizon, ends negotiations, and thereby excludes the possibility of a future change in affairs.

These aporias reveal justice as something that is never simply given, here and now, in a fulfilled presence. Justice itself transcends the presence of a given decision—one that has been "arrived at"; from within the legal system, it points toward the future:

Justice remains, is yet, to come, *à venir*, . . . *à-venir*, the very dimension of an event irreducibly to come. It will always have it, this *à-venir*, and always has. Perhaps it is for this reason that justice, insofar as it is not just a juridical or political concept, opens up for *l'avenir* the transformation, the recasting or refounding of law and politics. [. . .] There is an *avenir* for justice and there is no justice except to the degree that some event is possible which, as an event, exceeds calculation, rules, programs, anticipations and so forth.[21]

But if justice is not simply a juridical or political concept, what is it then? A philosophical concept—or even a theological one? One might understand it as a regulative idea in the sense of Kant—that is, as a concept of the highest order that admits no derivation, one that may guide action, but about whose reality nothing can be said. Likewise, one might understand it as a messianic promise. In *Specters of Marx* (1993), Derrida writes:

. . . what remains irreducible to any deconstruction, what remains as undeconstructible as the possibility itself of deconstruction is, perhaps, a certain experience of emancipatory promise; it is perhaps even the formality of a structural messianism, a messianism without religion, even [something] messianic without messianism, an idea of justice—which we distinguish from law or right and even from human rights—and an idea of democracy—which we distinguish from its current concept and from its determined predicates today [permit me to refer here to "Force of Law" and *The Other Heading*].[22]

In "Force of Law," Derrida formulates matters still more cautiously: "I would hesitate to assimilate this 'idea of justice' to a regulative idea (in the Kantian sense), to a messianic promise or to other horizons *of the same type*."[23] All the same, Derrida's writings from the 1990s circle time and again around the undeconstructible and the structure of a messianic or "quasi-messianic" temporality (one oriented on the future and emancipatory promise)—something messianic without messianism, without a messiah—as well as the question whether an "atheological heritage of the messianic"[24] is possible.

Some readers have seen Derrida returning to his Jewish roots here; examined from the standpoint of his later writings, deconstruction, on the whole, would therefore represent a form of negative theology. We should be cautious, however, for this would entail a return to forms of authenticity and identity that have previously been deconstructed, and it would mean affirming the very onto-theological inheritance that deconstruction was created to take apart. Until the end, Derrida evinced a critical attitude toward all forms of the theological and the religious, even if his writing occasionally took on a tone that invoked the numinous. At any rate, the second part of "Force of Law," which is devoted to a minute reading of Walter Benjamin's 1921 essay, "Critique of Violence," clearly rejects "neomessianical Jewish mysticism."[25]

Benjamin's text (which contains a nuanced argument that cannot be reproduced here, even approximately) reflects on the crisis of parliamentary democracy in the Weimar Republic—a crisis that fed, in 1933, into the National Socialist power-grab, which Benjamin viewed as the permanent contamination of law and violence. In the final instance, the aim of the text is to justify revolutionary violence: not as something that establishes (a new) law, but as a force that breaks through the mythical cycle of law and violence as a whole, and therefore overcomes law and the state altogether. (Benjamin takes inspiration, above all, from Georges Sorel's theory of the "proletarian general strike" which, unlike the "political general strike," does not seek a political power-change, but the ultimate destruction of state power.) Benjamin distinguishes between founding violence, "the one that institutes and positions law" (*rechtsetzende Gewalt*, "law-making violence"), violence "that maintains, confirms, and insures the permanence and enforceability of law" (*rechtserhaltende Gewalt*, "law-preserving violence"), and "the annihilating violence that destroys law" (*rechtsvernichtende Gewalt*, "law-destroying violence").[26] He calls the first two "mythical" (which, for Derrida, implicitly means "Greek"[27]); the latter he calls "divine" (which, for Derrida, implicitly means "Jewish"[28]). As the "principle of all divine end-making" (*Prinzip aller göttlichen Zwecksetzung*[29]), only law-destroying violence receives Benjamin's approval, whereas law-making and law-preserving violence remain inescapably stuck in the "magical," mythical circle of power.

Benjamin's essay is problematic, above all, because it establishes a connection between revolutionary violence and law-destroying, divine violence; thus, it declares that the destruction of "bare life" occurring in the name of such violence to be just(ified). Especially in light of the National Socialist regime and the Final Solution, Derrida observes that Benjamin's text contains a "terrible ethico-political ambiguity."[30] The ambiguity ultimately colors all political theology, whether it comes from the Left or the Right, for even a secularized doctrine of salvation justifies the elimination of law and the use of violence (the killing or sacrifice of life). Therefore, it is no coincidence that Benjamin, immediately after the publication of "Critique of Violence," received a "congratulatory letter"[31] from Carl Schmitt, a thinker of the so-called "Conservative Revolution." Derrida sees affinities between Benjamin and Schmitt—and Heidegger, too—which are founded in more than shared "hostility to parliamentary democracy, even to democracy as such, or to the *Aufklärung*":

Although Heideggerian *destruction* cannot be confused with the concept of destruction that was also at the center of Benjaminian thought, one may well ask oneself what such an obsessive thematic might signify and what it is preparing or anticipating between the two wars, all the more so in that, in every case, this destruction also sought to be the condition of an authentic tradition and memory, and of the reference to an originary language.[32]

This statement, which refers to Heidegger in particular, does not call for revision, but rather for precision on the part of deconstruction. The final words of "Force of Law" read:

This text ("Critique of Violence"—S.L.], like many others by Benjamin, is still too Heideggerian, too messianico-marxist or archeo-eschatological for me. I do not know whether from this nameless thing called the Final Solution one can draw something which still deserves the name of a lesson. But if there were a lesson to be drawn . . . the lesson that we can draw today . . . is that we must think, know, represent for ourselves, formalize, judge the possible complicity between all these discourses and the worst. . . . In my view, this defines a task and a responsibility the theme of which . . . I have not been able to read in either Benjaminian "destruction" or Heideggerian "*Destruktion*." It is the thought of difference between these destructions on the one hand and a deconstructive affirmation on the other that has guided me tonight in this reading. It is this thought that the memory of the Final Solution seems to me to dictate.[33]

Here, Derrida moves remarkably close to Adorno, who held that Hitler had "imposed" a categorical imperative on humanity—that people "arrange their thoughts and actions so that Auschwitz will not repeat itself, so that nothing similar will happen" (see the epigraph to this chapter).

It is possible to understand Derrida's conception of justice more fully on the basis of *this* "affinity," as well as his idiosyncratic maneuvering between the critique of religion and holding fast to *certain messianic figures.* If, *after Auschwitz,* it is necessary, on the one hand, to avoid the dangers that every political theology contains—that is, the destruction of the standing order or its justification *in the name* of a supposed "higher truth" or "more authentic authenticity" (whether of nation, race, the proletariat, or humanity)—on the other hand, it is just as important for criticism to preserve a standpoint external to the legal system and prevailing institutional forms, so that the deficiencies of the existing order can be named as such ("deconstructed") and another future can at least be *thought.* Derrida's insistence on the indeterminacy and futurity of justice responds to the first point; for him, it is neither possible nor permitted to declare any standing system or instance (be it a revolutionary movement, a political program, or a method of administrating justice or distributing goods) simply to be just, for this would necessarily occur at the price of justice itself. As for the second point, Derrida insists on holding firm to this concept, to the *matter,* of justice as *responsibility with respect to the Other,* even if it is infinite and can never be fulfilled. This involves, we can say with certainty, *a non-naïve figure of transcendence after Auschwitz,* after the "Death of God." It is a *figure of opening* that, in calculating and planning, in distributing and redistributing, in deciding and judging—in a word, within the present that remains trapped by the philosophical, political, and theological history of metaphysics—reveals another order to human affairs.

3.2 The Promise of the Gift
and the Gift of the Promise

Having determined that the possibility of justice rests upon responsibility with regard to the Other, Derrida, in his works of the 1990s, explored the (related) matters of the gift, friendship, hospitality, and democracy.

Counterfeit Money (1991) relates to "Force of Law" in conception and design insofar as it, too, insists on a hyperbolic figure that exceeds measure and economy. In this work, the figure of the gift stands at issue. The figure is not new for Derrida, even if its centrality is. Already in "Force of Law," the irreducible matter of justice, which cannot be traced back to anything else, is viewed in connection with "the Other's coming as the singularity that is always Other," on the one hand, and "the demand of gift without exchange, without circulation, without recognition or gratitude, without economic circularity, without calculation and without rules, without reason and without rationality,"[34] on the other. The possibility of justice seems bound to the possibility of an offering beyond economic exchange; like justice, the gift defies understanding in terms of a stable system of give-and-take.

Counterfeit Money presents a reading of the famous essay by French ethnologist Marcel Mauss, *The Gift: The Form and Reason for Exchange in Archaic Societies* (1923/1924)—a standard work for scholars in the fields of anthropology, sociology, cultural studies, and ethnology. According to Mauss, exchange in so-called archaic societies represents an all-encompassing activity—a "total social fact" that possesses economic, juridical, moral, aesthetic, religious, mythological, and morphological dimensions that far exceed the exchange of commodities in the narrow sense. His study focuses on the question why gifts must be repaid in kind. Mauss's answer is that the gift possesses, beyond its material value, a symbolic function; it is a form of address from the giver to the receiver that obliges the latter to respond. Mauss examines this symbolic function not just in foreign cultures, but also in a European context (among the Romans and Greeks); in the course of discussion, matters gradually turn from "exotic" and ancient locales to present-day societies, where Mauss gauges the moral and economic aspects of gift-exchange. Mauss's foundational ethnographic study reveals the moral, psycho-economic principle of the gift as a matter of compulsion—something that creates debt and obligation. This permits him to analyze the principles of service, work, the welfare state, and charity. Claude Lévi-Strauss, elaborating on Mauss's findings, later declared the reciprocal exchange of complementary values to provide the universal structure for life in society, as evident in practices as different as trade in goods, marriage (trade in women), and language (trade in words).

Derrida's reading of Mauss turns against such an understanding of structural and unavoidable reciprocity, inasmuch as reciprocity, taken as a "total social fact," subordinates the whole of life in human communities to the economic rule of comparable and calculable values. Derrida points out that Mauss's grouping of phenomena (e.g., the practice of *potlatch*, ring exchange among the Kula, the ternary forms of gift-giving among the Maori) under a single heading must be called into question, since "for there to be a gift, there must be no reciprocity, return, exchange, countergift, or debt."[35] At first, this observation seems to correspond to colloquial and juridical conceptions of the gift (in contrast to the exchange of commodities); giving, as it is defined by law, means the free transfer of ownership of a thing or a right to another party, without the demand for anything in return. From this perspective, the gift is precisely what needs *not* to be reciprocated. Upon closer examination, however, the mere absence of reciprocation in material form does not, by any means, shut down the cycle of exchange. Even if, in a legal sense, I am not materially indebted to a party who has given me a present (e.g., money), I still owe him thanks (that is, a symbolic or psychic equivalent of something material). Thus, if I only ever accept invitations and never extend one in turn, I will sooner or later be considered stingy or anti-social (that is, I will pay with my social respectability, or social capital). My failure to extend an invitation will have become a "counter-gift" in its own right—a negative response to social interaction and mutual recognition. Even if I refuse to accept a present (for example, because I consider it inappropriate or want nothing to do with the giver and do not wish to stand in his debt), I have not broken with the cycle of reciprocity, for I have (indirectly) answered the giver and "interpreted" his gift through a symbolic act. (Possibly, I may feel guilty for having offended him.) The reciprocity of communication and indebtedness extends beyond law and economy in the restricted sense.

Derrida does not contest the social or psychic economies of obligation connected with the gift. On the contrary: he emphasizes that such connections are already evident on the level of grammar—"to give something to somebody" or "to receive something from somebody" already implies the perception of "something" as a gift and of "somebody" as the one who gives or takes. In the process, the notion of a gift without a counter-gift—without reciprocity, exchange, or debt—literally becomes a "matter of impossibility."

If Derrida, *contra* Mauss and the entire tradition that builds on his research, nevertheless insists on the "impossible matter" of a pure and radically asymmetrical gift which interrupts economic and symbolic exchange and the "logic of debt," he does so for reasons similar to those motivating the way he views justice. He seeks to stress a hyperbolic, excessive figure that transcends the cycle of economy—a surplus outside of exchange that makes the orderly *quid pro quo* or *do ut des* of things and words possible in the first place.

We are going to give ourselves over to and engage in the effort of thinking or rethinking a sort of transcendental illusion of the gift. [. . .] For finally, the overrunning of the circle by the gift, if there is any, does not lead to a simple, ineffable exteriority that puts the economy in motion. It is this exteriority that *engages* in the circle and makes it turn.[36]

The semantics of the gift and of giving—beyond Mauss and the "critique of political economy"—relates to still more in Derrida's work. For one, it leads (yet again) back to Heidegger, who conceives of giving and the gift as an event that discloses Being and the world: "*Es gibt*"— "there is that which gives," a key phrase in his philosophy—precedes all that exists in concrete form; therefore, it cannot be grasped as something that "merely" exists in the manner of everything else. The "*Es gibt*" points over and beyond isolated beings and the metaphysics of presence concealed therein. Before something can *be*—in the sense of a presently existing thing (which then can be passed along or exchanged for something else)—it must first "be given." But what is given? To begin with: Being and world. Being and world lie beyond what exists in everyday form and designate the space within which everyday objects can be revealed in the first place. How is this "space" of world and Being laid open? At least for

Yet justice is not only this surplus→ it is also respect for fairness + reciprocity the Heidegger of the later writings (*On the Way to Language* and *On Time and Being*), it is "the word," that is, language.

Heidegger takes distance from the linguistic conception of language as a medium of communication conceived in terms of sender and receiver. Such an instrumental understanding of language remains, as Derrida also emphasizes, stuck within the framework of the model of exchange: "Someone says/someone gives something." This metaphysical view presumes that subjects are, as it were, "pre-constituted," and that they dispose of language and things as readily available matter. For this to be possible at all, however, *language itself* must first be given to the subjects who exchange words or things. For Heidegger, then, language—"the word"— is the original gift:

> The word, too, belongs to what is there—perhaps not merely "too" but first of all, and even in such a way that the word, the nature of the word, conceals within itself that which gives being. If our thinking does justice to the matter, then we may never say of the word that it is, but rather that it gives—not in the sense that words are given by an "it," but that the word itself gives. The word itself is the giver. What does it give? To go by poetic experience and by the most ancient tradition of thinking, the word gives Being. Our thinking, then, would have to seek the word, the giver which itself is never given, in this "there is that which gives."[37]

In everyday speech, this fundamental quality of the gift of language passes largely unnoticed, because language *as* language is eclipsed in favor of the specific meaning it is charged with conveying. Only in situations that occur at its limits—for example, when one does not find the right word, or when "words fail"—can the character of language-as-gift, its world- and self-disclosing essence, be experienced *ex negativo* as it were (when "world" and "self" fade from view).

Without explicitly equating the gift with "the word" or language, Derrida takes up Heidegger's structure of the "*Es gibt*," which precedes all reciprocity—and, indeed, the very existence of subject and object. As soon as the subject begins to perceive itself as such, the gift is already annulled:

> The becoming-subject . . . reckons with itself, it enters into the realm of the calculable as subject. That is why, if there is a gift, it cannot take place between two subjects exchanging objects, things, or symbols. The question of the gift should therefore seek its place before any relation to the subject, before any conscious or unconscious relation to self of the subject—and that is indeed what happens

with Heidegger when he goes back before the determinations of Being as substantial being, subject, or object. One would even be tempted to say that a subject as such never gives or receives a gift. It is constituted, on the contrary, in view of dominating, through calculation and exchange, the mastery of this *hubris* or of this impossibility that is announced in the promise of the gift. There where there is subject and object, the gift would be excluded. A subject will never give an object to another subject. *But the subject and the object are arrested effects of the gift, arrests of the gift.*[38]

Just like justice, the gift is something of which one can never say that it *is* (present), but only that "it is given" (*dass es [sie] gibt*). Just as giving seems to precede exchange, justice seems to precede law as its condition of possibility. Let us recall:

Wherever one can replace, translate, determine the X of justice, one should say: deconstruction is possible, as impossible, to the extent (there) where *there is* (undeconstructible) X, thus to the extent (there) where *there is* (the undeconstructible).[39]

"Gift," then, would be one of the possible replacements or translations for the undeconstructible *X* of justice. Both justice and the gift are undeconstructible because they precede every possible instance of construction and, indeed, every instance of *destruction* and of *deconstruction*, too.

Without this "*Es gibt*," nothing at all would be given. However, when Derrida speaks of a "promise of justice" and a "promise of the gift," his words indicate that neither justice nor the gift are simply transcendental. If he explicitly declares of the gift that it, "overrunning . . . the circle" of economy," also "*engages* in the circle and makes it turn,"[40] one may also suppose that justice is an overrunning element *within* the law, and therefore not located somewhere beyond the law. At the same time, the expression "promise" points out that this engagement and presence are, yet again, linguistic in nature. Indeed, for Derrida, the meaning of the gift is linked not just with the Heideggerian "*Es gibt*," but also with a concept of the *performative*, which extends beyond the individual speech act and into the matter of promising.

The concept of the performative comes from the English philosopher J. L. Austin, the founder of speech act theory. A series of lectures, *How to Do Things with Words*, published in 1962 after his death, has provided the basis for numerous developments in linguistics and analytic philosophy (e.g., the works of John R. Searle), on the one hand,

and for discourse analysis and reflections by Derrida and Judith Butler, on the other.

Austin's distinction between constative and performative speech acts is unimposing at first, yet it has far-reaching consequences. Austin first observes that language can in no way be restricted to the classical constative (determining) functions of naming and describing; in addition, there are specific forms of expression with which we *perform actions*—that is, with which we *change reality*. Such performative acts include, for example, baptizing, solemnizing a marriage, betting, threatening, ordering, promising, forgiving, as well as condemning someone (in court) or opening a meeting. The fact that such actions are possible through speech places the classical philosophical distinction between knowing/recognizing and acting into question. It thereby makes "speaking" something to be understood as part of social interaction (i.e., contexts). For example, the viability of speech acts such as "I hereby baptize you *X*," "I pronounce you man and wife," or "I condemn the accused to five years of prison without probation" presupposes the existence of certain institutions (church, civil registry, court) and the institutional authority of the speaker to perform the "deed." However, even "private" speech acts such as threatening, promising, or betting owe their effectiveness to the fact that they establish certain social relations and imply a series of actions.

Derrida engaged with speech act theory early on, first in the essay, "Sign, Event, Context" (1971), then, a few years later, in a polemical debate with John R. Searle that was published in 1977 under the title *Limited Inc.* Searle had reproached Derrida for misunderstanding Austin entirely (cf. the Epilogue below). In "Sign, Event, Context," Derrida stresses the originality of Austin's project and places Austin in the company of Nietzsche, who likewise (if in different terms) emphasized the performative (that is, the reality-creating and -changing) power of speech (cf. First Approach). According to Derrida, Austin's concept of the performative does "not designate the transport or passage of a content of meaning, but in a way the communication of an original movement (to be defined in a *general theory of action*), an operation, and the production of an effect. To communicate, in the case of the performative, . . . would be to communicate a force by the impetus of a mark."[41]

But in a second step, Derrida criticizes the restrictions Austin (and, after him, Searle) imposes on performative speech acts—in particular, 1)

his demand that the *context* be entirely determinable and controllable, and, 2) his notion that the *content* of the act be wholly subordinate to intention. Because of these restrictions, Austin's understanding of speech acts remains stuck in the framework of a theory of instrumental communication and dependent on philosophical assumptions about consciousness. *Contra* Austin and Searle (and in a manner analogous to arguments advanced by Heidegger), Derrida attempts to demonstrate that the *performative* dimension of language extends far beyond what can be governed by intention alone. Indeed, before subjects may even be said to "have intentions"—before they can threaten, bet, promise, and so on—they must yield to the performativity of language, which, by definition, defies complete mastery on their part. This is the case, first, because no context can ever be determined fully. Moreover, while it is possible to describe the general rules under which, say, a baptism or a ceremony must occur in order to be effective, one can never know whether all the conditions defined by the rules have really been fulfilled in a given instance. Necessarily and by definition, empirical context is infinite; in addition, the concept of context as an external frame or set of limiting circumstances can never be adequate to a performative utterance. Derrida speaks here of an "inner . . . context . . . of the words used."[42] Such "inner contextuality" results from the general citability or iterability (repeatability) of signs, without which performative utterances would not be possible at all. I can only promise, bet, baptize, threaten, and so on, because others before me have promised, bet, baptized, threatened, and so on—because such language games as promising, betting, baptizing, threatening, etc., already exist. At the same time, every single event in language is discrete in itself and, furthermore, internally divided.

Derrida illustrates this state of affairs through the example of the promise—an example that is not chosen at random insofar as the *gift of promising* ultimately is revealed as the dimension in which the original *performativity* of language is located. Whoever makes a promise contracts himself to a future that necessarily escapes control. He does not know if he will be able to fulfill his promise, for he could die before he can make good on it, or the means to realize the promise may be found wanting. Likewise, the individual to whom a promise is made does not know whether the party who makes it "really means it"—whether he intends to fulfill the promise at all. This is true even when the "giver" and the "taker" of the promise know each other well and enjoy mutual trust. By definition, the speech act itself is not transparent to the intentions of the speaker. Lying, which can occur even with the best of intentions, is always possible—for example, when I make a promise in order not to disappoint someone or to place him in my debt (however unconsciously), or because what has been promised corresponds to my own desire, but not to that of the other party. Austin and Searle exclude all these "fallacies" from consideration as matters of secondary importance. If Derrida stresses them—and moreover insists that they are inherent in the act of promising—he does so because a promise that cannot fail would not be a promise at all. A promise whose fulfillment is a foregone conclusion is no promise, but a constative statement about a sequence of events that will occur. It is possible to formulate the foregoing differently, too: an element of *fiction* dwells within every promise—the anticipation of its going into fulfillment in the future; this aspect, *as such*, changes the relationship between the giver and the taker, *even if it never happens*.

Still more important than the indomitability and incalculability within promising *with regard to the future*, however, is the fact that, in a decisive way, a promise never has its origin in the intentions of the party who makes it. A promise does not "fall out of the sky"; it always already provides an *answer* to the claim of the Other *in a given situation*. The possibility of making a promise does not have its origin in me; rather, it comes to me (as a gift) from the Other—more specifically, from another person—who gives me the possibility to respond to him, in a singular, unique situation, with a promise; additionally, it comes from the Other that is language itself, which places both me and the other person in a position where promising is possible:

There is no language without the performative dimension of the promise; the minute I open my mouth I am in the promise. Even if I say that "I don't believe in truth," or whatever, the minute I open my mouth there is a "believe me" at work. Even when I lie, and perhaps especially when I lie, there is a "believe me" in play.[43]

Derrida calls this event of promising, which occurs in the very act of speaking and exists independent of any determinate content, a "messianic a priori," the promise (of an answer to come). It inhabits speaking as such—outside the intentions of parties who speak. Whether I like it or not, speaking entails responsibility (*Ver-antwortung*). It involves commitment (*Überantwortung*) to the address and claim (*An-spruch*) of the Other and the messianic structure of language, which situates both of us in positions of responsibility. Elsewhere, Derrida speaks of an "original affirmation" instead of a "messianic a priori"—a kind of foundational contract that is given with language itself and precedes all individual speech acts.

Counterfeit Money (which was originally a series of lectures) begins by pointing toward the contract that exists between Derrida and his listeners; this work also exemplifies the matter at hand:

> [There] is an unsigned but effected contract between us, indispensable to what is happening here, namely, that you accord, lend, or give some attention and some meaning to what I myself am doing by giving, for example, a lecture. This whole presupposition will remain indispensable at least for the *credit* that we accord each other, the faith or good faith that we lend each other, even if in a little while we were to argue and disagree about everything.[44]

As the re-sponsibility/re-sponding with respect to the Other that occurs through the gift of language, the promise proves a further possible translation of justice, and it is undeconstructible, too, since it precedes all particular utterances. When Derrida locates deconstruction, as the "experience of the impossible," in the "borderland" separating the undeconstructible "*Es gibt*" (of justice, the gift, and the promise) from what admits deconstruction (law, economy, and metaphysics), he affirms that deconstruction has to bear witness to figures of the impossible: what is excessive, overrunning, and incommensurable. The final chapter will explore the form this program assumes in a deconstructive conception of the political.

Fourth Approach: Deconstruction and Democracy

> "Political ruin . . . results from the emergence of political bodies from the Family."
> —Hannah Arendt, "What is Politics?"

> "Peace is the state of differentiation without dominance, where differentiation involves participation."
> —Theodor W. Adorno, "On Subject and Object"

4.1 The Time of the Political

The path we have followed until now has led from the critique of metaphysical value-oppositions, through a deconstruction of patterns of thought predicated on the subject and consciousness, to the postulation of certain undeconstructible premises underlying deconstruction itself, which Derrida groups under the names of "justice," "the gift," "the Other," "hospitality," and "event." The trajectory can also be understood as a gradual shift away from a working-through of the metaphysical inheritance of the past toward the project of a future philosophy and a coming democracy. Derrida's more explicitly political writings of the 1990s (*Specters of Marx, The Other Heading, The Politics of Friendship, Rogues,* and *Philosophy in a Time of Terror*) unite both impulses—the first aiming for the deconstruction of the past, and the other directed toward projecting the future. However, we should observe right away that the two aspects of Derrida's thought cannot really be separated. It is impossible to do away with the past and then, as if on the *tabula rasa* of the present, invent a new and different future.

Let us recall: "There is no sense in doing without the concepts of metaphysics in order to shake metaphysics. We have no language—no syntax and no lexicon—which is foreign to this history; we can pronounce not a single destructive proposition which has not already had to slip into the form, the logic, and the implicit postulations of precisely what it seeks to contest."[1] The same holds for political thought, which participates in the same history. Moreover, the idea that one could first "overcome" the past and then turn to the future presupposes a metaphysical conception of time—a view that takes time as a series of "nows" that are strung together, as it were, in a series of presences. As we saw in our discussion of Heidegger (cf. above, 1.2), such a perspective does not correspond to the structure of Dasein, which should, instead, be viewed as the three dimensions of time existing *simultaneously*. To emphasize the contemporaneity of Dasein, Heidegger qualifies the being of Dasein as "care," which he glosses as "ahead-of-itself-already-being-in-a-world as Being-alongside (entities encountered within-the-world)" (*sich-vorweg-schon-sein-in-der-Welt-als Sein-bei [innerweltlich] begegnendem Seienden*).[2] Hereby, the sequence of determinations—future (*sich-vorweg*), past (*schon-sein-in*), and present (*sein-bei*)—implies a hierarchy.

An engagement with temporality also plays a significant role in Derrida's deconstruction of the metaphysics of presence. Just as the concept of *différance* contains an "original" delay that cannot be sublated in a past or future presence of "the thing itself" (cf. above, 2.2), so too, in later writings, does the inbuilt anachronism of the present's non-contemporaneity with itself assume significance. This occurs, above all, when Derrida discusses "inheritance" or the "structure of inheritance"—that which comes from the past yet also lies before us as a task and, for this reason, can never be fully appropriated:

I inherit something that I must also transmit: shocking or not, there is no right of property over inheritance. That's the paradox. I am always the tenant of an inheritance. Its trustee, its witness, or its relay. . . . I can't appropriate any heritage without remainder. Beginning with language. . . .[3]

"Beginning with language"—here, too, language is not a bequest among others; rather, it is what makes possible (and, at the same time, inevitable) acts of transmission, acts of memory and foresight. In short: language is what makes possible the simultaneity of the non-simultaneous; it is inheritance itself.

Hölderlin called language "the most dangerous of goods," given to man "that he bear witness to having inherited/what he is." Derrida quotes these fragmentary verses in *Specters of Marx*, which was written immediately after the collapse of the Soviet Union. This was a time when the world thought it had finished with Marx and Marxism. Marx could be forgotten, it seemed. When Derrida chose this moment to take up some of his writings (among others, *The Communist Manifesto, German Ideology,* and *The Eighteenth Brumaire of Louis Bonaparte*), he staged what he was talking about. Derrida's engagement with Marx marshaled the anachronic temporality of inheritance against an eschatological and teleological philosophy of history, whose adherents now believed they were witnessing the "coherent and directional History of Mankind" culminate in the victory of liberal democracy over socialism. Derrida writes of a neo-evangelic "gospel"[4] that announced the death of Marxism, exemplified by Francis Fukuyama's *The End of History and the Last Man* (1992)—a book in vogue at the time. Inasmuch as Fukuyama worked for the Rand Corporation and the administration of George Herbert Walker Bush, Derrida's intervention also concerned the question of how dominant discourses and ideologies come into being, and the ways that a new hegemonic order of the world was in the process of establishing itself in the United States.

Derrida saw danger not only in militancy and contempt for parties unwilling or unable to bow to the neoliberal program of salvation—by no means a small part of the world—but also in the potential this program held for repression. One of the book's main theses is that an inheritance that is not accepted, acknowledged, and taken up in a responsible manner returns in the form of ghosts. In the first place, then, "specters of Marx" occur in "all the forms of a haunting obsession that seems . . . to organize the *dominant* influence on discourse today. At a time when a new world disorder is attempting to install its neo-capitalism and neo-liberalism, no disavowal has managed to rid itself of all of Marx's ghosts. Hegemony still organizes the repression and thus the confirmation of a haunting. Haunting belongs to the structure of every hegemony."[5] Secondly, "specters of Marx" refers to the ghosts that haunted Marx himself—above all, "ghosts of the past" that threatened to "intoxicate" the nineteenth-century revolutionary project by turning it away from itself or turning it into a masquerade or a farce. For example, in the *Eighteenth Brumaire of Louis Bonaparte*, one reads:

Thus did Luther masquerade as the Apostle Paul; thus did the revolution of 1789–1814 drape itself alternately as Roman Republic and as Roman Empire; nor did the revolution of 1848 know what better to do than to parody at one time the year 1789, at another the revolutionary traditions of 1793–95.

[. . .]

The social revolution of the nineteenth century cannot draw its poetry from the past, it can draw that only from the future. It cannot start upon its work before it has stricken off all superstition concerning the past. Former revolutions required historic reminiscences in order to intoxicate themselves with their own issues. The revolution of the nineteenth century must let the dead bury their dead in order to reach its issue. With the former, the phrase surpasses the substance; with this one, the substance surpasses the phrase.[6]

Here, despite himself, Marx shares a linear and teleological conception of history with his own "gravediggers" in the twentieth century—the same parties who, in the name of a promise of the end of time, announce that "Marx must be forgotten" if we wish to arrive in the promised land of liberal democracy. In *structural* terms, the gospel of a liberal market economy and the gospel of communism are not as different as first appears. Marx, too, believed in the "end of history," which would arrive in the form of a "classless society." Like those who would bury him, he held a metaphysical conception of time, for he believed that one can make a clean slate by wiping away the past and achieving the fulfilled presence of one's "own substance." Such would be true "revolution."

Derrida, in contrast, insists that such adequation of the present to itself—under the banner of whatever ideology or eschatology it may be—can never occur. Quoting *Hamlet*, he observes that "the time is out of joint," irretrievably. Herein lies the structure of inheritance given with language. We *are* heirs, Derrida writes—and this means we are the heirs of Marx, too—whether we wish to be or not, and whether we know it or not. We live within Marx's legacy, and the legacy lives within us. It haunts us, and we *must* acknowledge and bear witness to it. Indeed, if we do not take up and take over the bequest of the past in a responsible manner, there can be no future, but only an empty repetition of the past. Therefore, the alternative does not involve recreating what has existed historically, or, alternately, making a fresh start. Rather, inheritance demands a critical choice:

An inheritance is never gathered together, it is never one with itself. Its presumed unity, if there is one, can consist only in the *injunction* to *reaffirm by choosing.* "One must" means *one must* filter, sift, criticize, one must sort out several different possibles that inhabit the same injunction. And inhabit it in a contradictory fashion around a secret. *If the readability of a legacy were given, natural, transparent, univocal, if it did not call for and at the same time defy interpretation, we would never have anything to inherit from it* [emphasis added]. We would be affected by it as by a cause—natural or genetic. One always inherits from a secret—which says, "read me, will you ever be able to do so?" The critical choice called for by any reaffirmation of the inheritance is also, like memory itself, the condition of finitude. The infinite does not inherit, and it does not pass itself on. The injunction itself (it always says "choose and decide from among what you inherit") can only be one by dividing itself, tearing itself apart, differing/deferring itself, by speaking at the same time several times—and in several voices.[7]

"Inheritance," for Derrida, does not mean passively receiving from the dead something that is automatically enriching or to be capitalized upon. Instead, "to inherit" is an active process that requires filtering, sieving, and criticizing—above all, *interpreting* and *reading.* Here, too, interpretation and reading refer to active processes that involve valuation and revaluation, displacement and change—processes that imply rejecting and forgetting, to be sure, but not ones that simply discard reading and interpretation *a priori* ("We can forget about Marx, there's no need to read him anymore"; "we can forget about Derrida"; "deconstruction is dead," etc.).

The concept of interpretation outlined here calls to mind both Nietzsche and Heidegger. When Heidegger, in "What is Philosophy?," calls the history of philosophy a "free succession" of interpretations, he points out that the kinds of thinking that have occurred in different epochs do not necessarily follow from each other in keeping with dialectical or teleological necessity; on the contrary, the event of transmission, appropriation, and passing-on an inheritance lies open at every point, and decision is always at issue. When Nietzsche calls interpretation a form of the will-to-power, the perspectivism of exegesis stands at issue just as much as the performative, reality-changing potential within it. Equally, it implies that "interpreting" does not mean the simple reading and expli-cation of texts. Understood in terms of an all-encompassing activity, interpretation involves all our ways of living with, and modes of acting upon, an inheritance—instances of appropriative transformation, out of the past and toward a future. In a further step—and in opposition to Heidegger's concept of "care" (in a certain measure)—Derrida declares that the "Being" of Dasein itself is inheriting:

Inheritance is never a *given*, it is always a task. It remains before us just as unques-tionably as we are heirs of Marxism, even before wanting or refusing to be, and, like all inheritors, we are in mourning. [. . .] *To be*, this word . . . means . . . to inherit. All the questions on the subject of being or of what is to be (or not to be) are questions of inheritance. There is no backward-looking fervor in this reminder, no traditionalist flavor. Reaction, reactionary, or reactive are but inter-pretations of the structure of inheritance. That we *are* heirs does not mean that we *have* or that we *receive* this or that, some inheritance that enriches us one day with this or that, but that the *being* of what we are *is* first of all inheritance, whether we like it or know it or not. And that, as Hölderlin said so well, we can only *bear witness* to it. To bear witness would be to bear witness to what we *are* insofar as we *inherit*, and that—here is the circle, here is the chance, or the finitude—we inherit the very thing that allows us to bear witness to it. As for Hölderlin, he calls this language, "the most dangerous of goods," given to man "so that he bears witness to having inherited/what he is [*damit er zeuge, was er sei/ geerbt zu haben*]."[8]

In this sense, we *are* the heirs of the best (of an emancipatory promise, which is historically connected with the political form of democracy), as well as the heirs of the worst (totalitarianism, wars, the camps of the Second World War). The task lies in assuming responsibility for this inheritance:

No justice—let us not say no law and once again we are not speaking here of laws—seems possible or thinkable without the principle of some *responsibility*, beyond all living present, within that which disjoins the living present, before the ghosts of those who are not yet born or who are already dead, be they vic-tims of wars, political or other kinds of violence, nationalist, racist, colonialist, sexist, or other kinds of exterminations, victims of the oppressions of capitalist imperialism or any of the forms of totalitarianism. Without this *non-contem-poraneity with itself of the living present*, without that which secretly unhinges it, without this responsibility and this respect for justice concerning those who *are not here*, of those who are no longer or who are not yet *present and living*, what sense would there be to ask the question "where?" "where tomorrow?" "whither?"[9]

The responsibility given with the structure of inheritance—or, better, the "responsibilization" of the present with respect to the past and the future—holds not just for readings and interpretations of philosophical and other texts (e.g., the works of Marx), but also for the critique of political forms, insofar as understanding them also has roots in the history of metaphysics.

4.2 Beyond Brotherhood (Politics of Friendship)

And in this great tradition there is not only a connected series of events but there is also progress. France has continued the Roman and Christian work that Christianity had promised, and France has delivered. *Brotherly equality* had been postponed to the next life, but she taught it as the law on earth to the whole world.

This nation has two very powerful qualities that *I do not find in any other.* She has both the principle and the legend: the idea made more comprehensive and more humane, and the tradition more connected and coherent.

This principle, this idea, which was buried in the Middle Ages under the dogma of grace, is called *brotherhood in the language of man.* . . .

This nation, considered thus as the asylum of the world, is much more than a nation. It is a living brotherhood.[10]

These words are not Derrida's, but belong to Jules Michelet, the great historian of the French Revolution and an ardent advocate of democracy. Derrida uses them as an epigraph in *Politics of Friendship* (a book that appeared in French in 1994 and was translated into English in 2006). It is important to understand *politics* in the plural here (as in the French title, *Politiques de l'amitié*), since, for Derrida, there always exist multiple politics. This brings us to our central item of concern. Derrida's "concept of the political"— which here (and elsewhere), stands in opposition to the thought of Carl Schmitt—rests upon the premise that the multiplicity of politics should in no way be mistaken for Politics with a capital "P" (that is, the activities of a state program or political *system*). Deconstruction can be understood as one of these politics, too—as a "politics of friendship," at that.

But why "beyond brotherhood"? What is it about the political figure of the brother, with *fraternité* as a political model, that makes it *the* political model for democracy? What does it mean to "deconstruct" this figure, and what ethical and political impulse animates such an act of deconstruction?

According to Derrida, one of the essential "gestures" of deconstruction is "not to naturalize what is not natural" (*de ne pas naturaliser ce qui n'est pas naturel*). In other words—and to sum up Derrida's argument—"brother" and "brotherliness" are figures that make the political into something natural that seems simply to be given; herein lie all the paradoxes of the modern nation-state.

The concept of politics rarely announces itself without some sort of adherence of the State to the family, without what we will call a *schematic* of filiation: stock, genus or species, sex (*Geschlecht*), blood, birth, nature, nation—autochthonal or not, tellurian or not. This is once again the abyssal question of the *phusis*. . . .

If no dialectic of the State ever breaks with what it supercedes [*relève*] and from which it arises [*ce dont elle relève*] (the *life* of the family and civil society), if politics never reduces within itself this adherence to familial generation, if any republican motto almost always associates fraternity with equality and freedom, as for democracy, it is rarely determined in the absence of confraternity or brotherhood.

Literally or through a figure, but why this figure?[11]

The quotation from Michelet provides an initial answer to the question. Carried by the pathos of what the Revolution has achieved, it celebrates the French nation as the "asylum" of a "principle" or an "idea" that Michelet calls "brotherly equality" and "living brotherhood." By casting events in these terms, Michelet inscribes the French nation into the history of progress—a *translatio imperii* that, in uninterrupted succession, passes from the Roman Empire, through medieval Christendom, into republican France. Michelet reads the history of progress both as the history of secularization *and* as a hegemonic claim: "France has continued the Roman and Christian work that Christianity had promised, and France has delivered. *Brotherly equality* had been postponed to the next life, but she taught it as the law on earth to the whole world."

But how can "brotherly equality" be prescribed without this command negating itself? If a nation gives the rest of the world the law of brotherly equality, does it not, through this hegemonic gesture, also break with the brotherly equality it demands? And what, exactly, is enjoined in the name of fraternity and the nation—in the appeal to a brotherly nation and national brotherliness? What does combining these two concepts or principles, the principle of brotherliness and the principle of nationality (or nativity), show?

Derrida's deconstructive project focuses on the hidden semantic potential of these concepts/principles and probes the contradictions inherent within them. In contrast to how matters may first appear, the way the state is conceived in modern democracies cannot be separated from the sphere of the *bodily* and *familial*, which provides the (imaginary) foundations of community. For modern citzens, the social body of the nation and "brotherliness" assume the function that the king's body and "fatherliness" once played with respect to royal subjects. However, nativity (in the sense of a place of birth and origin) and fraternity point away from the political space of democracy in the proper sense—anchored by writing in the constitution—toward a pre-political sphere still distinguished, as was the case in old-European monarchies, by the values of shared origin and consanguine relationships. If the foundational political narrative of modern democracy tells the story of a social contract, and if the basic model of the new society involves a contract between singular, independent, and autonomous individuals, nevertheless this mode of thinking remains shaped—in an ethno- and androcentric way—by the guiding values of "nativity" and "fraternity" (which, moreover, support increasingly marked affective investments). In other words, *foreigners* and *women* are still excluded—and more than ever—from the brotherhood of the republic.

"The anthropological schema is doing all the work here."[12] In other words, the values of a shared origin and love that is presumed "natural" are invoked in the name of brotherliness. Yet it is clear, as Derrida observes, that brotherliness extending *beyond* the family represents a matter of choice—a connection that can be terminated and must therefore be manifested and affirmed if it is to have substance and duration. No *natural* sign exists to prove that the Other is my brother. Moreover, inasmuch as words and feelings need not overlap, this is the case even where a biological brother is concerned: "The relation to the brother engages from the start with the order of the oath, of credit, of belief and of faith. The brother is never a fact."[13]

As a political model, then, brotherhood doubles or repeats the paradoxes that also distinguish the concept of the nation. Brotherhood must be produced politically, authenticated by signs, and "maintained" by public ceremonies. However, this can occur only inasmuch as brotherhood is conceived as the pre-political—and therefore "natural" and "substantive"—basis of the political. Here too, then—as in the case of the nation—the question of belonging arises. If one does not become a "brother" through the social contract, one must, on the one hand, already have been one (even without knowing or "remembering" it); on the other hand, being a brother requires active forms of *fraternization* (analogous to "nationalization") that make latent brotherhood manifest and/or differentiate the brother from the non-brother. Therefore, to the extent that brotherhood offers a regulative idea of the political, it oscillates between the pole of universal inclusion ("All men become brothers," as Schiller's paradigmatic *Ode to Joy* puts it) and, at the same time, the particularism of a community of shared ancestry or attitudes. Such a polarity between universal brotherliness and local, closed brother*hood* already distinguishes the Christian concept of fraternity. Both extremes also pervade the French Revolution. Thereby—and herein lies the central paradox of the model—the very claim to universality ultimately leads to the exclusion of ever-greater groups of the population from general fraternization. When revolutionaries dream of the "boundless city of Philadelphia" (etymologically, "brotherly love"), where all human beings form a single family, they pursue, at the same time, the progressive elimination of all parties who do not wish—or are unable—to conform to such universal harmony. First, the king is done away with, then the aristocrats, and, ultimately, a farraginous mass of "traitors" who do not share revolutionary ideals. The dialectic between brotherhood and suspicion leads to the fraternity's self-destruction from the inside. In the end, only the dead brother can be a "good" brother, for he alone cannot turn into a traitor.

Far from pacifying the nation or—for that matter, the human community—the very principle of brotherhood leads to an interminable division or splitting of the social body from within. The phantasm of homosocial autopoiesis comes to expression—and this, according to Derrida, is a kind of unthought and symptomatic feature at the root of all brotherhood. It is a matter of autopoiesis because the brothers are mutual midwives: by creating the revolution, they become their "own sons," so to speak. The process is homosocial because it is *brothers*—and not sisters, daughters, women, or anyone else—who create a community of equals, different from all others.

What the French Revolution gave especially vivid expression can, according to Derrida, be seen in the political model of brotherliness or fraternization in general—in the case of Greece and Rome, in medieval Christendom, and in modern democracies. It also occurs whether the "brother" in question bears this title or comes as a "friend"; the "friend," in Derrida's view, has always borne the traits of the brother in Western thought. (Thus, the greater part of the book on the "politics of friendship" is devoted to readings of philosophical treatises on friendship and politics from Aristotle, through Montaigne, up to Carl Schmitt; Derrida deconstructs the latter's distinction between friend and enemy as a criterion of the political.) The general concern of the book might be summarized as follows: since Aristotle, the political imaginary has presented the friend as a kind of brother; therefore, both the friend and the brother belong to a familial, fraternalistic, and therefore (phallo- or) androcentric configuration; perhaps today, this model is in the process of being overcome. "Let us dream," Derrida writes, "of a friendship which goes beyond the proximity of the congeneric double, beyond parenthood, the most as well as the least of parenthoods, when it leaves its signature, from the outset, on the name as on a double mirror of such a couple. Let us ask ourselves what would then be the politics of such a 'beyond the principle of fraternity.'"[14]

One possibility of moving "beyond brotherhood" would involve giving up the "old name," its logic, and, in renouncing it, embracing a politics of motherliness, of sisterliness, or simply of femininity. And why not? The *other* possibility—and this is the option that Derrida chooses—consists of retaining the inherited nomenclature and logic while *at the same time* decentering it, dislocating it, and introducing the "operation of a 'partisan.'"[15] In his view, "there is no choice":

If there were a single thesis to this essay, it would posit that there could be no choice: the decision would once again consist in deciding without excluding, in deciding without inventing other names and other concepts, in moving out *beyond this* [familial, fraternalistic, and androcentric, S.L.] politics without ceasing to intervene therein to transform it.[16]

It would not change much merely to set the "gynocracy" of sisterliness or motherliness against the andro-phallocentrism of brotherliness. Such an operation would remain indebted to the same values of familiarity, substantiality, and identity. Deconstruction, Derrida writes, must "necessarily [operate] from the inside, borrowing all the strategic and economic resources of subversion from the old [metaphysical] structure"[17] in order to decenter it *from within* and push it beyond its inherent limitations. Corresponding to the gesture of "demolition," of *de*construction, engagement with tradition must perform gestures of "building," of *con*struction. Indeed, in many ways, "deconstruction" means nothing but the simultaneity of these two contradictory and heterogeneous gestures. In this context, the "double gesture" of deconstruction

> would consist in not renouncing the logic of fraternization . . . all the while working to denaturalize the figure of the brother, his authority, his credit, his phantasm. The preference given to one or another fraternization (the democratic one) presupposes such work, presupposes that the brother figure not be a natural, substantial, essential, untouchable given. This same work would affect, in changing it, democratic fraternization—everything which, in democracy, still presupposes this natural fraternity, with all the risks and limits it imposes.[18]

The first movement of deconstruction involves laying bare paradoxes within the political model of brotherhood and drawing attention to the semantic latencies the concept entails, which haunt it (and, indeed, haunt the political community that uses the concept for orientation!). A second gesture displaces the notion of brotherhood and strips it of its ontological premises so that it may bear fruit for the principle of a "coming democracy" (*démocratie à venir*). Derrida addresses this principle—or thought— of a "coming democracy" in *Rogues: Two Essays on Reason* (among other works).

In *Rogues*, Derrida analyzes what he calls a "birth defect" of democracy—a paradox inherent in its *form* that is therefore inseparable from it. He also describes the dynamic as a "process of auto-immunization" (cf. below, 4.3). Here, we can again see the paradox of brotherhood we already observed, which lies in the fact that democracy must necessarily exclude those elements that endanger its existence. Insofar as the danger can only be banished by drawing boundaries of force through decisive action—an event that is necessarily undemocratic—both the operation of exclusion as well as its suspension amount to self-inflicted damage to the political form. As an example, Derrida cites the parliamentary elections in Algeria in 1992, which the Algerian government broke off out of fear that a victory by Islamic fundamentalists would menace democracy from within. Another instance that comes to mind are the Reichstag elections in Germany in 1933, which permitted Hitler to seize power in a fully democratic manner. Both processes—the suspended Algerian elections in 1992 and the completed elections in Germany in 1933—terminated in self-inflicted damage to the democratic system (which, in Germany, led to the system's complete collapse).

We should stress that, according to Derrida, the way democracy endangers itself—the vulnerability of this form of politics—is not an illness or defect to be remedied by political means. Instead—and as we have already observed—the problem inheres in the form itself, which is *necessarily* disposed to openness and uncertainty. In this regard, one can say that a permanent lack of authenticity, meaning, and identity characterizes democracy.

What is lacking in democracy is proper meaning, the very [*même*] meaning of the selfsame [*même*] (*ipse, metipse, metipsissimus, meisme*), the it-self [*soi-même*], the selfsame, the properly selfsame of the it-self. Democracy is defined, as is the very ideal of democracy, by this lack of the proper and the selfsame. [. . .] Which amounts to saying, . . . that there is no absolute paradigm, whether constitutive or constitutional, no absolutely intelligible idea, no *eidos*, no *idea* of democracy.[19]

This holds for democracy whether it is conceived as a Platonic "idea" or as a "regulative idea" in the sense of Kant. There is need to move beyond all such conceptions.

But then what—taking leave from any determinate or determinative form—is the sense of a "coming" or "future" democracy? The phrase *démocratie à venir*, which Derrida borrows from Maurice Blanchot, implies a kind of ethical imperative: it is not just a matter of a democracy that can or will perhaps arrive, but of one that *should* come.

In its constitutive autoimmunity . . . democracy has always wanted by turns and at the same time two incompatible things: it has wanted, on the one hand, to welcome people only on the condition that they be citizens, brothers, and compeers [*semblables*], excluding all the others, in particular bad citizens, rogues, noncitizens, all sorts of unlike and unrecognizable others, and, on the other hand, at the same time or by turns, it has wanted to open itself up, to offer hospitality, to all those excluded. But . . . it is adequate to democracy to do one or the other, sometimes one and the other, sometimes both at the same time and/or by turns. Rogues or degenerates [*les voyous ou les roués*] are sometimes brothers, citizens, compeers.[20]

The operative contradiction will become all the more pronounced, the more citizens, brothers, and equals identify with each other and the political community. The stronger the image of the authentic and the same, the greater the drive toward exclusion. At the same time, the desire for hospitality—for welcoming the excluded—grows stronger when patterns of internal identification become problematic, interrupted, and heterogeneous. If, in a certain sense, the contradiction of "autoimmunity" is inevitable, it is reinforced to a significant degree by all forms of self-affection, which express the desire for closure (i.e., exclusive and exclusionary identification). If, then, the phrase "democracy to come" does not refer to another democracy (whether archetypal or ideal) but to another *use* of democracy, it appeals to the reduction or suspension of community-founding identifications. Here, in contradistinction to brotherhood and shared participation in the similar and the equal, the democracy to come would designate an opening-up to the non-identical—a place of maximum heterogeneity without any common measure.

From this opening on, democracy would no longer be the regime of the brotherly and the identical, or of "living brotherhood" in the sense of Michelet, but the regime of everyone, beyond all exclusionary conditions. In this light, the future of democracy appears as the future of "the first to happen by":

Paulhan says somewhere, and I am here paraphrasing, that to think democracy is to think "the first to happen by" [*le premier venu*]: anyone, no matter who. . . . The first to happen by: is that not the best way to translate "the first to come"?[21]

Here, we encounter another leitmotif of Derrida's political thinking: the motif of hospitality (which he developed above all in *On Hospitality*, which engages with Emmanuel Levinas's ethics of alterity and Pierre Klossowski's trilogy of novels, *Laws of Hospitality*). The rule of "the first to happen by"—that is, in a certain sense, of the first to cross my path—also means the rule of unconditional hospitality extended to the Other or to the stranger. In this context, the stranger is conceived less as a "foreigner" or "asylum-seeker" (parties who are nothing but the counterpart of the "brother" or the "friend," as one who is *like* me or, indeed, consubstantial with me), but as the brother or neighbor himself whose "strangeness" or "otherness" demands recognition. "The first to happen by" can be anyone at all—the nearest and dearest, as well as the farthest away, the longtime resident or the newly arrived. Strangeness and foreignness are nothing that happens to a preconstituted identity from the outside (if so, they would fit seamlessly into the paradox of exclusion and hospitality already described). Rather, the matter is to be considered as a kind of original or anterior foreignness, one that precedes all territorial and familial positions. It would concern "a politics, a friendship, a justice which . . . begin where the beginning divides (itself) and differs, begin by marking an 'originary' heterogeneity that has already come and that alone can come, from the future, to open it up. If only unto itself."[22]

The double temporality indicated here characterizes the "prospectiveness" and the coming of a *démocratie à venir*. *On the one hand*, it involves the arrival or entry, here and now, of foreigners in the most concrete and political sense of the word—foreigners to whom the democratic community must open itself and afford hospitality without binding it to conditions of sameness, belonging, and brotherliness. *On the other hand*, it means for democracy to open itself, through its acceptance of the foreigner and the foreign, to itself and to its own future, that is, to the original lack of identity which determines its political form "beyond brotherhood" from within. This is the second sense of the temporality of the phrase "to come" (*à venir*): the foreigner and the foreign have always already arrived; they have always already unsettled all brotherly belonging, all certainty of a common origin or shared nature, and they have decentered it through their irreducible heterogeneity from within. It follows that the democracy to come and deconstruction intersect:

To be consistent with this de-naturalization of fraternal authority (or, if you prefer, with its "deconstruction"), a first necessity, a first law, must be taken into account: there has never been anything *natural* in the brother figure on whose features has so often been drawn the face of the friend. . . . De-naturalization was at work in the very formation of fraternity. This is why, among other premises, one must recall that the demand of a democracy to come is already what makes such a deconstruction possible. This demand is deconstruction at work. The relation to the brother engages from the start with the order of the oath, of credit, of belief and of faith. The brother is never a fact.[23]

From this perspective, "deconstruction" clearly offers more than an interpretive method among others—and more than a mode of reading or means of interrogating tradition critically. To be sure, it offers all this *too*—as much follows from the quotation above—but it also represents a movement that occurs within this tradition and within its philosophical and political forms themselves. "Deconstruction," then, as a mode of reading and as a scientific method, would both record and, at the same time, be part of another, more comprehensive process that, in taking place, opens tradition to its own political future. As such—as the future—it must necessarily remain undetermined; it is as undetermined as "the first person to happen by," who can only be my brother, my sister, or my friend *beyond* similarity, common origin, and shared substance.

4.3 Autoimmunity and the *Khôra* of the Democratic

The affirmation of the non-identical—the deconstruction of the values of the authentic, the "proper," and the proprietary—forms a leitmotif running through all of Derrida's works, from his philosophy of language, through the critique of ontology, and on to the later ethical and political writings. Derrida himself insisted that

there never was in the 1980s or 1990s, as has sometimes been claimed, a *political turn* or *ethical turn* in "deconstruction," at least not as I experience it. The thinking of the political has always been a thinking of *différance* and the thinking of différance always a thinking of the political, of the contours and limits of the political, especially around the enigma or the autoimmune *double bind* of the democratic.[24]

In conclusion, then, let us attempt to summarize the motifs. What Derrida says about the identity of political communities (whether speaking of the constitutionally secured democracies of Western nation-states, of Europe, or of the "world community") renews his analysis of the figure of auto-affection as "self-relation within self-difference"[25] which already characterized the structure of self-consciousness (cf. above, Second Approach):

What is proper to a culture is not to be identical to itself. Not to not have an identity, but not to be able to identify itself, to be able to say "me" or "we"; to be able to take the form of a subject only in the non-identity to itself or, if you prefer, only in the difference *with itself* [*avec soi*]. There is no culture or cultural identity without this difference *with itself.* . . .

This can be said, inversely or reciprocally, of all identity or all identification: there is no self-relation, no relation to oneself, no identification with oneself, without culture, but a culture of oneself *as* a culture *of* the other, a culture of the double genitive and of the *difference to oneself.* The grammar of the double genitive also signals that a culture never has a single origin. Monogenealogy would always be a mystification in the history of culture.[26]

This difference-to-itself, which holds together the "dwelling-place" of what is "with itself" and at the same time divides it, means something other than the endorsement of pluralism and multiculturalism that has become obligatory in the West. Indeed, it could be shown that these concepts *still* obey a traditional logic of identity insofar as they—even in rising above differences of origin, language, skin color, religion, and so on—affirm a shared substance (an "essence") of "man" or the human; this (supposedly) common basis turns the culture of the Other—or the Other of culture—into something proper and authentic, which "all of us" are meant to share. Less in reference to political or cultural communities than to religious ones, Derrida considers such ecumenical figures of reconciliation to belong to a covert strategy of Eurocentric colonialization.

In contrast to proponents of these views, Derrida is interested in an irreducible difference that not only separates "us" from "the others," but already divides every political or cultural community "from itself." The condition obtains, first, because of the anachronic temporality of the political, which comes with the structure of inheritance. Secondly, it stems from the structure of a *spatialization* that comes with—or, indeed, *as*—the political. Derrida calls this spatialization *khôra*. The word, from the Greek, means something like "occupied place" (as opposed to abstract space): "space that is occupied, an inhabited location, a demarcated place, rank, post, assigned position, territory, or region."[27] Yet at the same time, *khôra* is not the same as what "fills" it. Rather, it refers to something like the principle that provides space or place *tout court*—something that is itself formless and undetermined, and, for this reason, capable of assuming any form or determination at all. It is important to stress that it is "*something like*": not only is the word difficult to translate into other languages; it also refuses all definition inasmuch as it names what stands beyond definitions, period. In *Timaeus*, Plato uses the word to refer to the "third genus" (*triton genos*) that mediates between the Being of intelligible ideas ("archetypes") and the Becoming of physical things ("representations")—that which "[provides] a seat for all that has birth."[28] Plato calls *khôra* the "nurturer and wet-nurse of becoming"—that which takes things in and gives space to them. He compares it to malleable gold, upon which the smith confers shape, "since . . . it both always receives all things, and nowhere in any way has it ever taken on any shape similar to the ones that come into it; it is laid down by nature as a molding stuff for everything, being both moved and thoroughly configured by whatever things come into it; and because of these, it appears different at different times; and the figures that come into it and go out of it are always imitations of the things that *are* [i.e., the ideas], having been imprinted from them in some manner hard to tell of and wondrous."[29]

In confirmation of the fundamental indeterminacy of *khôra*, which Plato already qualifies as logically ungraspable and only to be described through images and analogies, interpretations of the term in the history of philosophy vary greatly. Most often, it is translated as "matter," "stuff," or "space." Derrida, on the other hand, takes the indeterminacy of *khôra* as his point of departure and refuses to translate the word. Neither a subject nor a substance, *khôra* can be given form and definition only insofar as it takes in form and definition and, in a concurrent gesture, gives them (a) space. Thus, Derrida's reading retains only the notion of an "irreducible spatialization" (*espacement irréductible*), of an "in-between" that precedes the appearance of something *as* something. We have already encountered this idea in the context of *différance*—the simultaneously spatializing and "temporalizing" (delaying) occurrence of *differentiation*, which must always already be in effect for differences between "positive elements" to become manifest. Under the name of *khôra*, Derrida takes up the notion again, which he first developed by analyzing differential articulation within the chain of signifiers.

Perhaps one might say that *khôra* "translates" the X of *différance* (just as we noted that "gift" and "promise" are translations of justice; cf. above).

Khôra, however, accentuates the spatializing aspect more strongly than the effect of temporalization. Derrida stresses that *khôra* stands before or outside of time (it is *pre-temporal*[30]); therefore, any attempt to determine its nature *within time* is doomed to anachronism. For this reason, one should perhaps consider *khôra* the precondition of *différance* and "*Es gibt*"—what makes room for the event of differentiation and the giving of the gift. *Khôra*, then, could only be *determined* by means of apophasis—a form of negative definition that only says what something is by saying what it is not:

> As something radically a-human and a-theological, *khôra* cannot even be said to occupy a place or to *be there* [*qu'il y a la khôra*]. The *there is* [*es gibt*] calls too much to mind the dispensation of God, Man, or even Being, as certain writings of Heidegger state ("es *gibt Sein*"). *Khôra* is not even this "it" (*es, ça*), the "it" of giving prior to all subjectivity.[31]

"Neither this nor that," but also not "both this and that": *khôra* oscillates between the twin poles of exclusion and participation. It invokes a "third genre" of discourse that does not obey the laws of logic and conceptual thought, yet it is not mythical or metaphorical. It involves thinking spatialization *before* all the metaphysical oppositions to which *khôra* gives place without belonging among them.

How much, then, is this irreducible spatialization associated with the political? A certain connection already appears in Plato's text. *Timaeus* begins with a prologue about the ideal state and the "right" or "best" way to fill political positions. The polysemousness of *khôra* always *also* implies questions concerning the relationship between (political) order and "location," the organization and the "furnishing" of the polis. Plato's text is already concerned with the matter of *genos*—kind, order, or "race"—the question about the place or territory assigned to each *genos* as its own sphere. Still today, "democracy . . . remains a model of intranational and intrastate political organization within the city";[32] in other words, its point of orientation is the idea of a *genos* (a people, nation, or cultural community), belonging to a certain territory. Nation and people (*gens*), for their part, imply the idea of common descendance (*natio*) and origin (genealogy) that mark a territory "of one's own." Even now, access to state citizenship—and therefore to civil rights—depends on the principle of origin and/or territory. Carl Schmitt, in particular, has emphasized that no arrangement of rights and politics can exist without claiming and "indenting" (*kerben*) space.

Khôra, while *making possible* this principle of territory, subverts it, too. Without its "irreducible spatialization," there would be no filling of places, no occupation or marking of space. Yet *khôra* also makes all occupation and marking something preliminary, inauthentic, and revocable. Already in Plato's *Timaeus*, a certain contradiction arises between the rigid order of the ideal state, as it is first invoked, and *khôra* as the "third kind" between being and becoming, which, as a "wandering cause," receives no place itself, but for this same reason can assume any form. *Khôra* is that which separates every place from itself. In *Rogues*, Derrida combines the thought that occurs under the name of *khôra* with the syntagm of a "coming democracy"—which, therefore, one might perhaps call the "third genre" of the political: "the democracy to come would be like the *khôra* of the political,"[33] the spatializing opening-up of the political to itself and to its own future. The space of the political has to be thought in a different way; the principles of nation-state, territory, and sovereignty must be overcome.

Today, this process seems to be underway already under the name of "globalization." The liberalization of world commerce, the digital revolution, the connection and mixing of cultures, the globalization of telecommunications networks, the increasing significance of international institutions and contracts represent so many steps toward de-nationalization. Yet at the same time, globalization does not necessarily imply democratization or greater social justice. Derrida points out that never before in the history of mankind have violence, inequality, exclusion, hunger, and economic oppression affected as many people as now:

Instead of singing the advent of the ideal of liberal democracy and of the capitalist market in the euphoria of the end of history, instead of celebrating the "end of ideologies" and the end of the great emancipatory discourses, let us never neglect this obvious macroscopic fact, made up of innumerable singular sites of suffering: no degree of progress allows one to ignore that never before, in absolute figures, never have so many men, women, and children been subjugated, starved, or exterminated on the earth.[34]

Globalization plays a key role in international financial and economic crises, unemployment, economic wars, the massive increase of migration from the Third World into the First (as well as corresponding streams of deportation), mounting international debt, the expansion of the armaments industry and weapons trade, the dissemination of nuclear weapons, and international terrorism (which classic conceptions of war and civil war no longer adequately explain).

The collapse of the Soviet Union and the end of the Cold War seem to have meant an opening of political borders and, therefore, a chance for a "New International" of world politics. However, since September 11, 2001, at the latest, we have faced another division of international political space, with corresponding images of the enemy. Derrida's thinking of the political unfolds between these two large-scale events. The side he chooses is that of continued internationalization in the name of democracy—the side of "an extension of the democratic beyond nation-state sovereignty, beyond citizenship," "the creation of an international juridico-political space that, without doing away with every reference to sovereignty, never stops innovating and inventing new distributions and forms of sharing, new divisions of sovereignty. (I refer to *inventing* here because the to-come gestures not only toward the coming of the other but toward inventions—invention not of the event but through the event.)"[35] Derrida prefers to speak of "mondialisation" rather than globalization because the world (*le monde*) and the worldly, as opposed to the globe (*le globe*) and the global, preserve the memory of European history and therefore inscribe themselves in a structure of inheritance. Moreover, the Latin word *globus* (ball) connotes the self-containment and self-sufficiency of a circle or a sphere; it suggests the idea of the Earth as a holistic unity and, for this reason, a total or totalizing conception of political space. In contrast, "world" (*monde*) points back to the Latin *mundus*, "which in an Abrahamic (Jewish—Christian—Muslim, but above all Christian, tradition) designates a particular continuum of time and space extending toward a history where all men are brothers—in the language of Paul, 'world citizens': fellow human beings and neighbors insofar as they are all creatures and children of the same God."[36]

This may sound surprising in terms of what has been said about the deconstruction of fraternity (cf. above, 4.2). However, when discussing globalization or mondialisation, Derrida's political gesture involves retaining the "old names" and betting on their transformability. What holds true for the "brother" holds true for the "world," and it holds true for democracy itself. *Here, too, it is necessary to choose by inheriting*:

> Is it still in the name of democracy, of a democracy to come, that one will attempt to deconstruct a concept, all the predicates associated with the massively dominant concept of democracy, that in whose heritage one inevitably meets again the law of birth, the natural or "national" law, the law of homophilia or of autochthony, . . . and so forth?
>
> What remains or still resists in the deconstructed (or deconstructible) concept of democracy which guides us endlessly? Which orders us not only to engage a deconstruction but to keep the old name? And to deconstruct further in the name of a *democracy* to come? That is to say, further, which enjoins us still to inherit from what—forgotten, repressed, misunderstood, or unthought in the "old" concept and throughout its history—would still be on the watch, giving off signs or symptoms of a stance of survival coming through all the old and tired features?[37]

What resides in the "old" conception of democracy—and what, today, is perhaps "coming into its own"—would be the twofold principle of inherent self-deconstruction *and* the universalization that this "inborn" quality makes possible. Here lies, too, the connection between mondialisation *as a European project* and the "old name" of democracy. The matter involves

> the absolute and intrinsic historicity of the only system that welcomes in itself, in its very concept, that expression of autoimmunity called the right to self-critique and perfectibility. Democracy is the only system, the only constitutional paradigm, in which, in principle, one has or assumes the right to criticize everything publicly, including the idea of democracy, its concept, its history, and its name. *Including the idea of the constitutional paradigm that is universalizable, whence its chance and its fragility.* But in order for this historicity—unique among all political systems—to be complete, it must be freed not only from the [regulative] Idea in the Kantian sense but from all teleology, all onto-theo-teleology.[38]

Derrida calls democracy's immanent principle of self-criticism or self-deconstruction an "autoimmune process"—the ability to treat parts of the "own" body as "foreign" and reject them, or, conversely, to accept foreign matter *like* or *as* something that belongs to it. The expression occurs in later writings when he displaces the lines demarcating the "proper" and the "foreign":

The process of auto-immunization . . . [that] interests us particularly here . . . consists for a living organism, as is well known . . . , of protecting itself against its self-protection by destroying its own immune system. As the phenomenon of these antibodies is extended to a broader zone of pathology and as one resorts increasingly to the positive virtues of immuno-depressants destined to limit the mechanisms of rejection and to facilitate the tolerance of certain organ transplants, we feel ourselves authorized to speak of a sort of general logic of auto-immunization.[39]

This choice of words to describe the principle of immanent democratic self-critique does not, at first glance, seem particularly felicitous. It connotes not only biological (and therefore natural) processes, but also pathological ones, which call to mind an ill-omened tradition of the "organic" in metaphors of state and community; these figures, in turn, are associated with submetaphors of parasitical social pathology, representations of social conflicts as "illnesses" within the "social body," and so on—precisely the kind of thing at which deconstruction otherwise takes aim. Derrida seems to employ these words for *strategic* reasons. The formula of democratic "autoimmunity" serves polemical ends inasmuch as it opposes classical notions of auto-nomy (self-rule or self-determination) and, by the same token, the tautological discourse of selfness and sameness—circular closure upon and within itself—as the foundation of democracy. Like globalization, the classical conception of democracy ("government of the people, by the people, for the people") implies the solipsism of a circle or sphere:

It seems difficult to think the desire for or the naming of any democratic space without what is called in Latin a *rota*, that is, without rotation or rolling, without the roundness or rotating rondure of something round that turns round in circles, without the circularity . . . of some automobilic and autonomic turn or, rather, return to self, toward the self and upon the self; indeed, it seems difficult to think such a desire for or naming of democratic space without the rotary motion of some quasi-circular return or rotation toward the origin itself, toward and upon the self of the origin, whenever it is a question, for example, of sovereign self-determination, of the autonomy of the self, of the *ipse*, namely, of the one-self that gives itself its own law, of autofinality, autotely, self-relation as being in view of the self, beginning by the self without the end of self in view—so many figures and movements that I will call from now on, to save time and speak quickly, to speak in round terms, *ipseity* in general.[40]

The circular *ipse* or *autos* of auto-nomy designates both the self-sufficiency of sovereign consciousness and the principle of nation-state sovereignty. Just as unconditional as it is indivisible, it relies on the model of the auto-affecting subject. Democracy based on the principle of national popular sovereignty, just like the globe of globalization, has the form of a circle or sphere. "The people"—Derrida quotes from Alexis de Tocqueville's famous *Democracy in America*—"reign over the American political world as God rules over the universe. It is the cause and the end of all things; everything rises out of it and is absorbed back into it."[41]

However, this classical form of democracy "clashes with . . . another truth of the democratic, namely, the truth of the Other, heterogeneity, the heteronomic and the dissymmetric, disseminal multiplicity, the anonymous 'anyone,' the 'no matter who,' the indeterminate 'each one.'"[42] This "other truth" continually hinders and interrupts the closing of the circle—the tautological auto-affection and auto-affirmation of the people—and makes democracy "more than one" and "minus one."[43] Thereby, the circle transforms into an ellipse—which means that it becomes both an incomplete syntagm (an ellipsis) as well as a (stretched) circle with more than one focus. Such simultaneity of—or such simultaneous desire for—inclusion *and* exclusion of the heteronymous makes democracy a political form that is at once dynamic, expansive, fragile, auto-deconstructive, indeterminate, and universalizable. The form is autoimmune—as opposed to autonomous—insofar as its inherent, permanent self-criticism can both reject what "belongs" to it as its "own" and absorb what is "foreign" to it. Today, the self-deconstructive aspect of democracy would, above all, consist in detaching both democratic practices and the concept or idea of democracy from everything that still ties them to the values of territory, the nation, sovereignty, origin, the people as a community of shared ancestry, the familiarity of the familial, the "homeland," and so on. Accordingly, opening-up to heterogeneity stands at issue in all questions pertaining to citizenship, rights of entry and residence, border patrol, asylum rights, voting rights, civil rights for "foreigners," and so on. At the same time, the doubly "autoimmune" process is the movement by which the democratic itself is mondialized insofar as this does not mean the homogenizing hegemonialization of the globe by a dominant form of life and ideology, but "the potential for universalization beyond the State and the nation, a universalization that would universalize nothing but the taking-account of anonymous and irreducible singularities."[44] Because its difference has infinite dimensions, it is "indifferent to any particular difference, to the raging quest for identity corrupting the most indestructible desires of the idiom."[45]

In addition to the problems produced by deregulation in the spheres of economy and law, international crime, the uncontrollable proliferation of nuclear arms, and so on, Derrida maintains that the process faces danger on a political level for two further reasons. The first involves an "archaic phantasm" and an "archaic conception" of community—the nation-state, sovereignty, borders, blood, and soil—as evidenced, in particular, by ethnic wars (in the Balkans and elsewhere). The weakening of state sovereignty and the collapse of large-scale political territories always entail the "globalization of regionalisms," the "Balkanization" of the world, the multiplication of local communities rallying to the signs of a primeval "ontopology" of presence. "By *ontopology* we mean an axiomatics linking indissociably the ontological value of present-being [*on*] to its *situation*, to the stable and presentable determination of a locality, the *topos* of territory, native soil, city, body in general."[46]

Today, the ontopology of local communities is "outdated" because of "tele-technological dislocation," which itself repeats an originary dislocation:

All stability in a place being but a stabilization or a sedentarization, it will have to have been necessary that the local differance, the spacing of a *displacement* gives the movement its start. And gives place and gives rise [*donne lieu*]. All national rootedness, for example, is rooted first of all in the memory or the anxiety of a displaced—or displaceable—population. It is not only time that is "out of joint," but space, space in time, spacing.[47]

The "raging quest" of regional "affirmations of identity" occurs in fear of the return—the trauma—of irreducible spatialization that has always already taken place. The other factor threatening the process of mondialisation is even more complex, for it concerns the European origin ("rootedness") of the process itself. "Despite a fortunate perfectibility, despite . . . undeniable progress," institutions of international law suffer from "at least two restrictions":

The first and most radical of the two stems from the fact that their norms, their charter, the definition of their mission depend on a certain historical culture.

They cannot be dissociated from certain European philosophical concepts, and notably from a concept of State or national sovereignty whose genealogical closure is more and more evident, not only in a theoretico-juridical or speculative fashion, but concretely, practically, and practically quotidian. Another limit is strictly linked to the first: this supposedly universal international law remains, in its application, largely dominated by particular nation-states.[48]

Because it is bound to Roman-Christian culture, mondialisation today still means "Europeanization." However, just as the political institution of democracy delimits itself and detaches from particularized, national sites, "Europe," too, has begun to deconstruct itself. For this reason, the mondialisation of "the European" also signifies an objection to Eurocentrism. Eurocentric mondialisation experiences a crisis in its autoimmune system inasmuch as the attempt to establish it worldwide entails losing resistance to transformation and change:

What is exported, in a European language, immediately sees itself called into question again in the name of what was potentially at work in this European legacy itself, in the name of a possible auto-hetero-deconstruction. Or even, I would say, of autoimmunity. Europe is in my opinion the most beautiful example, and also the allegory, of autoimmunity.[49]

The logic of autoimmunity, already at work within the European legacy itself, irresistibly leads to the universal demand that its own origin be deterritorialized and de-historicized, that its borders and hegemony be contested. For the same reason, the form and the concept of democracy, which constitute the core of the European legacy, cannot stand fixed or still as a regulative idea or an ideal. If one foresees a goal or "end" to the historical changes that are underway, the horizon closes again and the democracy to come—as the *khôra* of the political—once more becomes a hegemonic space that is invested in such-and-such-a-way, usurped by a particular idiom.

If, today, "duty dictates assuming the European—and uniquely European heritage of . . . democracy," then one must also

[recognize] that this idea, like that of international law, is never simply given, that its status is not even that of a regulative idea in the Kantian sense, but rather something that remains to be thought and to come [*à venir*]: not something that is certain to happen tomorrow, not the democracy (national or international, state or trans-state) of the future, but a democracy that must have the structure of a promise—and thus the memory of that which carries the future, the to-come, here and now.[50]

Khôra, one might say, names the space of the political itself insofar as it is open and therefore democratic. *Khôra* signifies the openness of the public realm—the "between" of irreducible spatialization before and beyond all positive determination.

Since the attacks on September 11, 2001, the openness of the public—and therefore of the political itself—has been threatened by a new closing of the world and division into ideological camps. According to Derrida, the situation is "worse than the Cold War" because the logic of friend and enemy, domestic and foreign, good and evil, which (again) prevails can never rise to the task of mastering the reality of so-called "international terrorism." Not only do all classical distinctions between interstate war and partisan combat, civil war and terror, founder here; the very distinction between domestic and foreign, which they presuppose, does, too:

Those called "terrorists" are not, in this context, "others," absolute others whom we, as "Westerners," can no longer understand. We must not forget that they were often recruited, trained, and even armed, and, for a long time, in various Western ways by a Western world that itself, in the course of its ancient as well as very recent history, invented the word, the techniques, and the "politics" of "terrorism."[51]

Equally, it is impossible to make out "states," "groups," or "cultures" to which responsibility for terrorism can be unequivocally assigned—neither "Arabs" in general, nor "Islam" as such, nor the Arab-Islamic Middle East are to blame. Each one of these formations is internally heterogeneous, full of tensions, conflicts, and contradictions. The same holds true for the so-called "West": the coalition that formed when the United States initiated the "War on Terror" is impermanent and heterogeneous: "It is not only Western, and the 'front' without front of this 'war' without war does not pit the West against the East or against the Far East . . . , or the Middle East, where every country condemned, more or less sincerely, the terrorism and agreed to fight it."[52]

If a "front" in this war can be identified at all, according to Derrida, it concerns the confrontation of two political theologies: on the one hand, that of America, where despite a theoretical separation between church and state, strong biblical (above all, Christian) themes—from refrains of "God bless America" to talk of the "Axis of Evil," and on to the call for "Operation Infinite Justice"—pervade official political discourse; on the other hand, there is an "enemy" identified as Islamic, extremist, and fundamentalist. Yet caution is advised here, too, for *both* political theologies, Derrida observes, "[issue from] the same stock or common soil of what I would call an 'Abrahamitic' revelation.'"[53] For this reason, it is extremely significant that the epicenter of all these "wars" is located, at least metonymically, in the conflict between Israel and Palestine—between a "democracy that has not yet cut the umbilical cord with religious, indeed with ethnoreligious, authority" and "a virtual Palestinian state . . . that, in preparing its constitution, has not yet given up on declaring Islam the official state religion."[54]

To the extent that the political theologies combating each other may be characterized as "enemy brothers" (Christianity, Judaism, and Islam all invoke Abraham as their common ancestor and thereby lay claim to the "promised land" that God promised to his descendants for the ages), the logic of autoimmunity, which is otherwise the motor of political transformation, seems to assume suicidal traits. In the context of the "War on Terror" and the religious identifications that underlie it (or serve as an alibi), it no longer seems to be a matter of making the domestic foreign and rejecting it from oneself; nor is what is supposedly foreign (terror, "terrorists," or "Islam") accepted as one's own. Derrida suggests as much, at any rate, in *Philosophy in a Time of Terror*, when he interprets the attacks of September 11 as a symptom of "suicidal autoimmunity."[55] By this, he means not just the suicide bombers, who employed their own bodies as weapons, but also the suicide of those who "often recruited, trained, and even armed" them[56]—which is to say, first and foremost, the United States. Derrida speaks of a "monstrous" or "perverse" autoimmunity, both on the part of "Islamic fundamentalists" who repudiate their belonging to techno-capitalist modernity, and on the part of the United States, which does not acknowledge that its weapons and wars have made "terrorism" possible.

In this context, Derrida once again places his hope in "Europe," or, more precisely, in a potential difference between a "new shape of Europe" and the United States. What distinguishes the European model of mondialisation is, not least of all, a historically unique separation both between church and state, and, even more importantly, between political discourse and every kind of religious doctrine—something that exists neither in the Arab or the Muslim world, nor in the Far East, nor in America.

"Mondialisation," then, does not mean just the independence of democracy from the nation-state and the creation of international political-juridical space; it also possesses a decisive element of secularism, rootedness in *this* world, which deconstructs the theological and religious inheritance that forms part of the ontology of substance and (self-)presence just as much as political history, properly speaking.

The process of such self-deconstruction as mondialisation, of mondialisation as self-deconstruction of the European inheritance (be it philosophical, political, "cultural," or "religious") is not, by any stretch of the imagination, complete. Indeed, it can never be complete—it *can* and *must* never be complete—if the political is to remain open. In Derrida's view, it is not least of all philosophers who face the task it implies:

Though I am incapable of knowing who today deserves the name philosopher (I would not simply accept certain professional or organizational criteria), I would be tempted to call philosophers those who, in the future, reflect in a responsible fashion on these questions and demand accountability from those in charge of public discourse, those responsible for the language and institutions of international law. A "philosopher" (actually I would prefer to say "philosopher-deconstructor") would be someone who analyzes and then draws the practical and effective consequences of the relationship between our philosophical heritage and the structure of the still dominant juridico-political system that is so clearly undergoing mutation.[57]

This is exactly what Derrida himself undertook, from the patient analyses of *Grammatology*, by way of *Margins of Philosophy*, up to the positions he articulated concerning recent political events. The horizon of his thought, the question of difference and its institution in a coming democracy, remains open. Derrida's legacy (his legacy, too) must now be taken up by us. And so, wherever we are, we must begin there. *Somewhere, wherever we are:* in a text where we already believe ourselves to be—for example, in this one, here.

Epilogue: Deconstruction in America / America in Deconstruction

In order to speak of "deconstruction in America," one would have to claim to know what one is talking about, and first of all what is meant or defined by the word "America." Just what is America in this context? Were I not so frequently associated with this adventure of deconstruction, I would risk, with a smile, the following hypothesis: America *is* deconstruction *[L'Amérique, mais c'est la decon-struction]*. In this hypothesis, America would be the proper name of deconstruction in progress, its family name, its toponomy, its language and its place, its principal residence. [. . .] But we have learned from "deconstruction" to suspend these always hasty attributions of proper names. My *hypothesis* must thus be abandoned. No, "deconstruction" is not a proper name, nor is America the proper name of deconstruction. Let us say instead: deconstruction and America are two open sets which intersect partially according to an allegorico-metonymic figure. In this fiction of truth, "America" would be the title of a new novel on the history of deconstruction and the deconstruction of history.[1]

To take a shortcut and get very quickly to the point, I will distinguish two times in my work, two recent upheavals. The one and the other had their place, their landscape, as well as their language, in this country, in the East and then in the West, in New York and in California. [. . .]

The first, about which I will only say a word, was on the occasion of a colloquium organized by Drucilla Cornell at the Cardozo Law School around the theme "Deconstruction and the Possibility of Justice." In "Force of Law" I tried to demonstrate that justice, in the most unheard-of sense of this word, was the unde-constructible itself, thus another name of deconstruction. [. . .]

And last spring, once again in the United States, on the other side, on the other coast, on the occasion of a keynote address that I was generously invited to deliver at a large colloquium, "Whither Marxism" at the University of California, River-side, I was finally able to hazard a discourse that would have liked to be something other than a Marxist discourse, something other than a reading *on* Marx or a read-ing *of* Marx, in the conventional, academic, or exegetical sense of the word. What I try to make understood there corresponds first to a political position-taking: it was uttered first of all *in* America, but surely also *on the subject of* America, and doubt-less, to an extent that remains to be determined, *against* a certain America in the new world order that is attempting to impose itself today.[2]

Deconstruction is more than one language.[3]

It is impossible to provide a comprehensive and concise overview of the fortunes of deconstruction in America here. The matter would require another book—or even several. Today, what one might call "deconstruc-tive elements" (or "elements of deconstruction") are found in literary the-ory, postcolonial studies, critical legal studies, feminist theory, philosophy, history, and other disciplines—to say nothing of discourses outside aca-demia. It is impossible to survey everything, especially since the "fields" themselves—that is, academic disciplines as well-defined, circumscribed entities—are now all in a "state of deconstruction."

Such an enterprise would amount to "squaring the circle" for other reasons, too. For one, circumstances prohibit a neat distinction between "production" and "reception"—and in more than one sense. Beginning in 1967, Derrida regularly taught in the United States. He did so first at Johns Hopkins, then—from 1975 on—at Yale; starting in 1989, he taught in New York. From 1986 until his death, Derrida also lectured at the Uni-versity of California, Irvine, where his papers now reside. Derrida wrote, at least in part, *in* America, *for* America, and *in confrontation with* certain currents of Anglo-American philosophy. Especially after the end of the Cold War, his works also took aim "*against* a certain America in the new world order . . . that is attempting to impose itself today." After a certain point, that is, the difference between Europe and the United States was inscribed both in his critical activities and in the way his texts circulated.

Second, Derrida's stateside readers should not be described as "recip-ients"—as "followers" who simply adopted his "method" and propagated it in their own country. (The book at hand has discussed, in numer-ous ways, the fact that deconstruction represents neither a method nor a "school" in the conventional sense.) Rather, fellow scholars who took on critical impulses in Derrida's writings developed their own modes of "deconstruction"—that is, distinct deconstructive practices of reading. In so doing, they disseminated his theory and transformed it, in ways it is impossible to survey in comprehensive fashion. As J. Hillis Miller—one of the so-called "Yale Critics"—observed:

"Method" is not at all the same thing as "exemplary acts of reading," which is what I would claim they [Jacques Derrida and Paul de Man] *do* provide. You can learn quite a bit, to speak in litotes, about how to read by reading Derrida and de Man. Of course no one, certainly not I, could claim to match them in rigor and insight. But that does not relieve me (or anyone else) from the responsibility to try. I am obliged to try to read as well as they do. This does not mean reading as they do. No example or presupposed theory can help me with that.[4]

Third, individual readings, like original works of criticism, are never shaped or informed by a *single* author, "school," "method," or "model." All that a given critic has read or encountered—"acts of reading" that s/he considers "exemplary"—will "influence" his or her particular approach. Scholars who have been "influenced" by Derrida may also have read Foucault, Lacan, or Barthes (to say nothing of other thinkers) and been "influenced" by them. Any list of authors "influenced by deconstruction"—such as one readily finds online—should be taken with a grain of salt; there is no need to repeat them here.

Instead, I will briefly sketch three points of encounter (instead of "influences") which, in my estimation, represent crucial intersections between "deconstruction" and "America." Were one to make a truth of fiction, one might refer to these meetings as so many chapters in a novel about the history of deconstruction. At the same time, a different story might be told, or the same story might be told differently. My choice is partial at best, and it results from personal experience. I present the viewpoint of a European scholar and reader of literature who has certainly been "influenced" by Derrida, but also by others. Although trained in the Continental tradition of thought, I lived and worked in the United States for several years; recently, I returned to Europe. Curiously enough, most of this short book was written in Chicago—albeit in German, and for German readers. The epilogue, on the other hand, has been written in Munich—in English, and for American readers. It is impossible for my American experiences not to enter the equation—my own encounters in and with the "States of Theory," as Derrida once called the United States, and with the "lines of amity and enmity" that traverse them.

1. Deconstruction Meets New Criticism:
The Emergence of "Theory"

Europeans are always struck by the fact that what they know simply as "philosophy" is called "Continental philosophy" or, alternately, "the history of philosophy" in the United States; the latter title in particular makes their philosophy seem to be a matter of primarily antiquarian interest—something distinct from "real" philosophy. Conversely, Americans may be surprised to learn that what they consider "real" philosophy is called "analytic philosophy" in Europe—an Anglo-American peculiarity with a limited scope (even though, over the course of the last ten or twenty years, analytic philosophy has spread more and more abroad). If one accepts these distinctions, however, Derrida's thought clearly belongs to "Continental philosophy"—in terms of geographical provenance, the traditions to which it is indebted, and "style." Continental philosophy is more commonly taught in literature departments than in philosophy departments in the United States. Accordingly, literature departments have represented the most important sites of reception not just for deconstruction, but also, more generally, for French philosophy from the 1950s to the 1990s; that is, they have provided key sites of exchange for structuralism and poststructuralism. In a polemical turn against such labeling (indeed, even against academic philosophy itself), the intersecting currents—and the productions to which they have given rise—have also simply been called "theory," without any accompanying adjective.

In this context, a sort of foundational event occurred at the so-called "structuralism conference" that was held in Baltimore in 1966 and has been famous ever since. At the newly founded Humanities Center at Johns Hopkins University, Richard Macksey and Eugenio Donato gathered—under the banner of "The Languages of Criticism and the Sciences of Man"—all the thinkers of note, more or less, from France who were as yet unknown in the United States. The aim of the conference was to acquaint the American public with the structuralist paradigm and its influence on critical methods in humanistic and social studies. Parties invited included René Girard, Roland Barthes, Jacques Lacan—and Jacques Derrida.

The meeting unfolded differently than anticipated, due to the fact (among other things) that structuralism no longer dominated the intellectual scene in France entirely. Derrida's lecture—"Structure, Sign and Play in the Discourse of the Human Sciences"—for example, critiqued the thinking of Ferdinand de Saussure and Claude Lévi-Strauss and already pointed toward what would become known as "poststructuralism." Accordingly, the second edition of the conference proceedings (published in 1972) was no longer named after the event itself, but was entitled *The Structuralist Controversy.*

At this gathering, Derrida met Paul de Man for the first time. Independently, de Man had developed his own brand of deconstruction. The two thinkers remained friends until the latter died in 1983. De Man, who was born in Belgium in 1919 and emigrated to the United States in 1952, became one of the most important mediators between European and American criticism. After earning a Ph.D. from Harvard in the late 1950s, he held positions at Cornell, Johns Hopkins, and the University of Zurich before being appointed, in 1970, Professor of French and Comparative Literature at Yale. Here—along with Geoffrey Hartman, J. Hillis Miller, and Harold Bloom—de Man numbered among the so-called "Yale Critics" (alternately, the "Yale School of Literary Criticism"), whose representatives were indebted to Derrida and deconstruction in various ways.

The "Yale Critics" did not constitute a homogeneous school, however, and they are certainly not to be viewed as Derrida's "disciples"—that is, as parties who imported and disseminated Derrida's "method" in the United States. The late 1960s and early 1970s should instead be viewed as a time when different developments—academic, cultural, and (last but not least) political lines of division—intersected and created a climate favorable to the reception of "French theory" (as it is sometimes also known). The particular thinking of difference it offered led American scholars with extremely different backgrounds to develop their own, independent intellectual projects.

Around 1970, departments of literature in the United States were still largely shaped by the authentically American school of "New Criticism," which emphasized close reading. The Yale Critics had also been trained in this approach. Close reading—the examination of literary texts with as much attention to detail as possible—certainly connects New Criticism and deconstruction (on deconstruction as a practice of reading, cf. Chapter 2), however, the underlying assumptions changed under the auspices of "French theory." In particular, notions concerning language, meaning, and the unity and autonomy of the "work" underwent modification. New Criticism had held the meaning of texts to be "objective"; language was deemed immanent and therefore a matter dependent neither on authorial intention nor on the reader's sensibilities. New Criticism viewed literary form as something closed unto itself—unified and autarchic; once completed, it was held to stand independent of the social and historical conditions of its emergence. Accordingly, the critic's task was to bracket all factors external to the text and to disclose the relationships between its ideas and form. New Critics may have found tension, irony, or paradox in these relations, but they aimed at resolving them into unity and coherence of meaning. Moreover, New Criticism also sought to be a *science* of literature, with a technical vocabulary ensuring objectivity and the general validity of interpretation.

Deconstruction challenged this conception of texts and how one should read them. In the first place, it argued, written works—including literary ones—cannot be autarchic and self-contained because, as constructs of language, they are conditioned by the general iterability (repeatability) of signs. Every linguistic sign is, to a certain degree, always already a quotation; likewise, every text forms part of a context and refers to other contexts, whose kind and number can never be exhaustively determined. (This consideration has been developed above all by the theory of intertextuality.)

Second—and as a matter of due consequence—no text possesses a unified or stable meaning. Texts can neither be controlled completely by the intention of the author nor are they "objectively" anchored in a linguistic structure. This already follows from Saussure's conception of language as articulation (cf. above, 1.4), which Derrida took up and radicalized. The ineluctable polysemousness and ambiguity of linguistic signs, however, also demand that *readings* not fix the text in terms of the unambiguous contents of its supposedly "objective" meaning. A text—and especially a literary one—does not constitute an organic whole in which all formal elements ultimately yield a unified and coherent meaning. Rather, it is comparable to an open web that points beyond its own borders; different threads ("signifying structures") can be taken up and followed—which, as Derrida says, "must be *produced* by reading in the first place" (cf. above,

2.1). It does not follow that reading constitutes an arbitrary process. However, it does mean that—based on context and the interest(s) the reader brings to the work—it is both possible and valid to read the same text in different ways. Accordingly, it is no longer a matter of finding the "right" ("objective") interpretation, but rather of situating the text in the context of a specific field of inquiry that must first be explicated; only in this way can one make it "speak." (Above all, the implications of this line of thinking have been developed by reader-response criticism.)

Finally—and, once again, following on the preceding—readings in a "deconstructive" mode operate with textual tensions, contradictions, and paradoxes in a different way than those that follow the method of New Criticism. Now, points of incoherence and contradiction are not understood as faults or mistakes that the reading should solve or sublate into a higher unity, but as symptoms of an aesthetic conflict or epochal set of problems that the text either registers or enacts, with or without the intention of the author. As Derrida's reading of Rousseau exemplifies (cf. above, 2.4), the most revealing points in a text are its lines of rupture—the places where it says something other than what it does, where it subverts its own logical premises or aesthetic procedure and enters into conflict with itself.

On this level, too, the work of art is *recontextualized* by deconstruction: it occupies a position in literary and aesthetic—social and political—history. It controls this history less than it is controlled by it. Let us recall:

> The writer writes *in* a language and *in* a logic whose proper system, laws, and life his discourse by definition cannot dominate absolutely. He uses them only by letting himself, after a fashion and up to a point, be governed by the system. And the reading must always aim at a certain relationship, unperceived by the writer, between what he commands and what he does not command of the patterns of the language that he uses. This relationship is not a certain quantitative distribution of shadow and light, of weakness or of force, by a signifying structure that critical reading should *produce*.[5]

As is well known, New Criticism originated in the economically underdeveloped American South, "in the region of traditional blood and breeding where the young T.S. Eliot had gained an early glimpse of . . . organic society."[6] One need not be a Marxist to discern certain structural parallels between the backward-looking conception of society of the Southern

Agrarians and their conception of the literary work. In either sphere, "coherence" and "integration" offer the key points of reference. Needless to say, such unity and organic wholeness are purchased by bracketing contradictions, denying differences, and enforcing segregation (racial segregation in society and politics, segregation of art and society in the realm of aesthetics).

The political implications of New Criticism do not stand at issue here; they represent a topic to be addressed separately. It is necessary to mention the matter, however, in order to appreciate that theoretical controversies and political confrontations often cannot be separated: theoretical issues in the humanities do not just represent matters of general abstraction, but also involve ideological climates that express a certain understanding of human beings, society, scholarship, the university, and so on. In this sense, then, the controversies surrounding New Criticism and deconstruction in the 1960s and 1970s may be viewed alongside pioneering political struggles that occurred around the same time: the Civil Rights Movement, protest against the war in Vietnam, student movements, the fight for women's and minority rights, and so on. In broad terms, deconstruction opposes a theory and politics of non-belonging—of difference and the non-identical—to the politics of identity and belonging advanced by New Criticism (among other approaches). That said, deconstruction is not a theory of literature first and foremost, nor may it be reduced to one; what is more, its effects have hardly been limited to literary scholarship.

In the 1970s and 1980s, departments of literature assumed the role of advancing interdisciplinary study. Jonathan Culler described their new function as follows in 1986:

The major critical development of the past 20 years in America has been the impact of various theoretical perspectives and discourses: linguistics, psychoanalysis, feminism, structuralism, deconstruction. A corollary of this has been the expansion of the domain of literary studies to include many concerns previously remote from it. In most American universities today a course on Freud is more likely to be offered in the English or French Department than in the Psychology Department; Nietzsche, Sartre, Gadamer, Heidegger, and Derrida are more often discussed by teachers of literature than teachers of philosophy; Saussure is neglected by linguists and appreciated by students and teachers of literature. The writings of authors such as these fall into a miscellaneous genre whose most convenient designation is simply "theory," which today has come to refer to works that succeed in challenging and reorienting thinking in fields other than those to which they ostensibly belong, because their analyses of language, or mind, or history, or culture offer novel and persuasive accounts of signification.[7]

If Derrida himself called this interdisciplinary development an "effect of deconstruction," he in no way meant that his "theory" or "method" had caused it. Rather, he was referring to the fact that "deconstruction"—by moving beyond boundaries of genre, destabilizing fields of identity, and challenging scholars to think outside disciplinary confines—was already occurring in many places anyway, whether this name was employed or not, and not just in departments of literature. For all that—at least in 1986—he thought the "turn" was particularly pronounced in the United States. With this in mind—at a conference that was held the same year at the University of California, Irvine—Derrida spoke of the United States as the "States of Theory"; in so doing, he expressed the hope that the political efficacy of "theory" might extend beyond the ivory towers of academia.

2. Deconstruction Meets Speech Act Theory: Politics of the Performative

Indeed, many articulations of theory which take up Derrida's thinking (among other intellectual projects) advance explicitly political claims. Examples include postcolonial studies, which critique the ethnocentrism of Western Thought (e.g., Homi K. Bhabha and Gayatri Chakravorty Spivak—who wrote a dissertation under Paul de Man and translated Derrida's *Grammatology* into English), the philosophical writings of Judith Butler (who studied at Yale and established a new foundation for feminist theory with her critical deconstruction of sexual difference), and certain branches of critical legal studies (which, along with literary studies and philosophy, represent the third field where deconstruction has taken root).

What proves decisive for these new theoretical orientations is the insistence on the *performativity* not only of scholarly, but also of legal, and even everyday discourses and distinctions—a matter that Derrida himself addressed, at the latest from 1971 on (cf. above, 3.2). This concept merits renewed mention here because it provides a point of reference shared by many authors who are readers of Derrida; moreover, it occasioned an important debate that occurred in the United States: Derrida's polemical exchange with the philosopher John R. Searle in 1977.[8] The embittered argument illustrates the fault lines between Continental philosophy (or, more precisely, a certain kind of Continental philosophy) and Anglo-American (or analytic) philosophy. The fundamental divisions concern different conceptions of language and subjectivity. Are linguistic expressions performative in general (Derrida), or just a clearly defined class of utterances (Searle)? Can the intentionality of the speaking subject fully govern the linguistic actions it performs (Searle), or not (Derrida)? The first question concerns the potential of language to depict reality as it is—and therefore the possibility of scientific objectivity. The second involves the sovereignty of the speaking subject—consciousness itself.

What is more, the debate between Searle and Derrida illustrates the different modes of reading that follow from their opposing philosophical positions. Reading J. L. Austin's *How to Do Things With Words*—the foundational work of speech-act theory—Derrida offers a prime example of deconstruction in action: on the one hand, he derives his conception of the performative from Austin's text, but at the same time, he works through the contradictions inherent in the way Austin presents the concept (which, in all fairness, Austin himself notes with precision—e.g., questioning his own distinctions, changing or displacing key terms, etc.). Derrida does not seek to demonstrate Austin's "mistakes" or to improve his system, but to uncover the unvoiced logocentric assumptions on which his reflections are based—assumptions that articulate themselves in terminological difficulties. Ultimately, his aim is to displace and radicalize Austin's own conception of the performative—that is, "to go beyond Austin with Austin," as it were. Derrida pursues a course of *active* reading that neither claims to be uniquely correct (even though he seeks to convince the reader, of course), nor means to uncover Austin's true intention; rather, his point is to appropriate the text in a critical and selective fashion and, by this means, to develop distinctions of his own to critical ends.

Searle, in contrast—as one gathers from his response to Derrida—proceeds from an entirely different set of assumptions. He claims that Derrida "has failed to discuss the central theses in Austin's theory of language," that "he has misunderstood and misstated Austin's position at several crucial points,"[9] and that he "has a distressing penchant for saying things that are obviously false."[10] In short, Searle alleges that Derrida has "misinterpreted Austin."[11] Such claims presume that a *correct* interpretation of the text exists (i.e., Searle's own); Derrida's reading—insofar as it deviates from the "true" meaning—can only be false. Moreover, Searle makes what Austin *wanted* to say—his intention (which, of course, can only be identified by means of interpretation, i.e., by reading)—the standard of judgment. Insofar as Derrida does not share these assumptions, Searle's "refutation" misses the point entirely. The affect-laden tone (why is a deviant reading of a text "distressing"? For whom? For the guardians of an imperiled orthodoxy?) points to the stakes of the debate, however— and for Derrida, too, whose response to Searle strikes a similar note.

For one, the stakes involve affirming institutional positions—that is, control of what counts as accepted knowledge or a scientific paradigm; as a corollary, the matter concerns what is deemed proper or improper for instruction at universities. Secondly, what stands at issue is the same *performative power of language* that occasioned the debate. Asserting one's own interpretation as the only one that is "correct"—establishing it as orthodoxy, so that the act of interpretation is no longer perceived as such, but rather counts as the simple truth—with respect to a text, authorial intentions, a state of affairs, or anything else: that *is* the performative force of language, connected with a will-to-power caught up in contexts and genealogies. Fortunately, it is difficult today—under conditions that are to some extent democratic (even if the concept of "democracy" remains problematic; cf. Chapter 4)—for a single party to erect his or her interpretation as the uncontested truth.

The performative feature of language—the power to *create* a reality, to establish an interpretation as truth—provides the object of analysis for many writers whose projects have taken up Derrida's thought. To take a single—but significant—example, *Excitable Speech: A Politics of the Performative*, by Judith Butler, examines the phenomenon of linguistic vulnerability in instances of hate speech or fighting words. Butler investigates the power of language and discourse in general to produce, in the first place, what it supposedly simply names—that is, the power both to constitute and to alter social identity. "One is not simply fixed by the name one is called," Butler writes. Rather, in being called an injurious name, one is derogated and demeaned. But the name holds out another possibility as well: by being called a name, one is also, paradoxically, given a certain possibility for social existence, initiated into a temporal life of language that exceeds the prior purposes that animate that call. Thus the injurious address may appear to fix or paralyze the one it hails, but it may also produce an unexpected and enabling response. If to be addressed is to be interpellated, then the offensive call runs the risk of inaugurating a subject in speech who comes to use language to counter the offensive call.[12]

On the basis of the ambiguity of "name-calling" (whether such names are injurious or proper—or simply matters of prevalent distinctions in social discourse, e.g., "male," "female," "gay," "lesbian," and so on), Butler formulates strategies of linguistic "mis-" or "re"-appropriation in order to counter the operations of the original speech acts. (The best-known example of this strategy is probably the reappropriation of the label "queer"—originally an anti-gay epithet—by gender minorities who are not heterosexual, heteronormative, or gender-binary.) "Those who argue that hate speech produces a 'victim class,'" Butler argues, "deny critical agency and tend to support an intervention in which agency is fully assumed by the state. In the place of state-sponsored censorship, a social and cultural struggle of language takes place in which agency is derived from injury, and injury countered through that very derivation."[13]

Postcolonial thinkers such as Homi K. Bhabha and Gayatri Spivak employ similar strategies when they "deconstruct" prevalent oppositions such as Orient-Occident, Christianity-Islam, and periphery-center; by situating themselves in a middle-position, they challenge the polarizing narratives of imperialism. "The terms of cultural engagement, whether antagonistic or affiliative, are produced performatively," Bhabha writes in *The Location of Culture*: "The representation of difference must not be hastily read as the reflection of *pre-given* ethnic or cultural traits set in the fixed tablet of tradition."[14]

But if these—and other—politics of the performative are "influenced" by Derrida, they are also indebted to other currents of "French theory" (above all, to Michel Foucault and Jacques Lacan) and to Anglo-American speech-act theory. What is more, their engagement with deconstruction neither excludes disagreement with Derrida (Gayatri Spivak's reading of Marx, for example, differs considerably from Derrida's), nor does it impede the coining of new concepts and ideas. For all that, deconstruction and advanced types of gender theory and post-colonialism find a common ground in critiquing occidental metaphysics and essentialism (that is, what Derrida described as logocentrism, phallocentrism, and ethnocentrism) and in a shared understanding of language in terms of performative force (whether addressing theory or daily life and politics).

The same holds for currents within critical legal studies that engage with deconstruction. By definition, the field of law is concerned with performatives, since verdicts ("I hereby adjudge the defendant guilty as charged and sentence him to five years of prison") represent an instance of language that constitutes action in the narrow (Austinian) sense. Verdicts do what they say, and they do so *only* by saying so: there is no other way to sentence a defendant than to pronounce the verdict, which is then carried out solely on the basis of what has been said—provided, of course, that the verdict itself has been pronounced under the "correct" circumstances, which involve the authorization of the person who pronounces judgment and an array of institutional and procedural requirements (i.e., everything that, with Austin, counts as the cultural and institutional "context" for this speech act in particular).

As we saw in Chapter 1, Derrida's critique of metaphysics in the wake of Nietzsche and Heidegger first unfolded as a critique of language and the form of judgment. It implies the interminability (*Unabschließbarkeit*) of context(s)—the fact that every judgment, with respect to the individual or particular case to be assessed, must, fundamentally and inevitably, also be *unjust*. This holds consequences for judicial decisions insofar as they represent a special type of institutionalized judgment—that is: a judgment invested with authoritative force. In the introduction to *Derrida and Legal Philosophy*, Peter Goodrich, Florian Hoffmann, Michel Rosenfeld, and Cornelia Vismann observe:

Derrida's significance for legal thought begins with his early readings of Nietzsche and the radical revision not simply of the concept of truth as a metaphor but of language, and specifically of sentences as judgments. [. . .] If all sentences are judgments and if judgments are necessarily sentences, how can we ever escape being sentenced, judged again and again by law? The answer to the omnipresence of sentences, the longing not to be sentenced, the desire to defer deciding, to resist knowing in advance, was the initial impetus and the definition of deconstruction which posed the endlessly non-authorial question of what the sentence did not say, could not judge, let free. In legal terms this meant at the very least that positive law did not and could not say everything. The fact of its textuality, the inevitable polysemy of language, meant that meaning also escaped law and hence that justice was only possible as a subtext or implicit future on the margins of the extant norm.[15]

According to Goodrich, insistence on the textuality of law means, first of all, performing a return to philology—whereby "philology" involves, in both the Nietzschean and the Derridean senses of the term, "the art of reading well—to be able to read out facts *without* falsifying them by interpretation and *without* losing caution, patience, delicacy, in the desire to understand."[16] Such philological practice Goodrich calls "grammatology" (and not "deconstruction," which, for him, is "no more than a device by which terms of art are unpacked by reference to their history and the semantic context of their use"[17]). He remarks that "grammatology received neither welcome nor exposition in the [American] legal academy until it was reiterated by Derrida, in a somewhat different form, in a now famous article on deconstruction as justice ["Force of Law"; cf. Chapter 3], published initially in a law review in 1990."[18] It was only then that

[s]uddenly, charismatically, and not without a certain radicalism, deconstruction was relevant to law: It marked a space of nonjudgment, a moment of suspension of law, the unique instance of undecidability in which prior norms give way to the singular act of decision. The name of this theoretical space of excess, this beyond of law that deconstruction marked, was simply "justice."[19]

But if grammatology means the suspension of the law, undecidability, and a space of non-judgment—"philology as *ephexis* [restraint] in interpretation"[20]— what does this mean concretely, at court, for example, where decisions *have* to be made, where interpretation and judgment cannot be postponed endlessly?

According to Goodrich, the implications are twofold. On the one hand, grammatology requires a certain ethics of decision-making on the part of the judge:

The ethics of grammatology lie in attending to the face, to singularity, to the words and gestures that are actually used. [. . .] Ethics necessitates the interruption of the rote and repetition of precedent and the other habits that make up the past of law. To do justice means looking and listening, engaging with and attending to what is unique and struggling to presence in the plea, call, or case that the judge must hear.[21]

In other words: passing judgment should never represent a mechanical act of subsumption or automated application of a norm to a "case." Furthermore, the interruption of rote activity—of affirming precedents and repeating other habits—requires knowledge of the history of law, that is, of the mechanisms of legal transmission. The future of grammatology, as Goodrich sees it, lies in the study of the material conditions of possibility of law, past and present. These material conditions derive from writing systems and their politics of power. Yet at the same time, they are not limited to books or writing in the conventional sense. Rather, they include other media and their specific modes of inscription:

> The opening pages of *Of Grammatology* were concerned not with the fixity, longevity, or permanence of the book. Rather, they addressed a long-term shift in the meaning of inscription or writing. The history of writing moved from inscriptions upon the body, to inscriptions upon other skins—upon "wethers" or texts—and thence to print and now to screen. Technology, and specifically the videosphere, has expanded the range and scope of social inscriptions and so of the representations of law. [. . .] The grammatology to come, the work of interpreting the images, the bodies and performances that make up the increasingly extravagant public sphere of law, is precisely a question of attending to the details of these new forms. It is a question of viewing these embodiments, these newly visible performances of legality as nonaccidental signs. What are the details of the images and bodies relayed? Which gender performances, racial identities, or corporate norms make up the videosphere of law? At the very least, and risking a pun, it makes sense to hypothesize that neither the scholar nor the judge is any longer usefully blindfolded in the domain of law.[22]

3. Deconstruction Meets Pragmatism: A Pragrammatology to Come

"The United States, the land of plain English and straight talking—Europe without brakes."[23]

Derrida's concern with the performativity of speech acts and their institutional settings—especially problems of justice—also points to certain affinities between deconstruction and pragmatism. In the afterword to *Limited Inc.* (his exchange with Searle), Derrida insists on the difference between indeterminacy and undecidability. "[U]ndecidability," he declares, "is always a *determinate* oscillation between possibilities (for example of meaning, but also of acts)"; these possibilities themselves are "*pragmatically* determined," that is, "highly *determined* in strictly *defined* situations" (e.g., determined by contexts that are discursive—syntactical or rhetorical—as well as political, ethical, etc.).[24] In this sense, he adds that "grammatology has always been a sort of pragmatics," even though "the discipline which bears this name today involves too many presuppositions requiring deconstruction, very much like speech act theory, to be simply homogeneous with that which is announced in *De la grammatologie*. A pra[gma-]grammatology (to come) would articulate in a more fruitful and more rigorous manner these two discourses."[25]

When he wrote these words, Derrida most likely had in mind what is usually called "neopragmatism" or "linguistic pragmatism"—a philosophical orientation associated above all with the works of Richard Rorty. Indeed, Derrida and Rorty shared an anti-essentialist outlook that led both of them to reject foundationalist conceptions of philosophy. In the absence of any verifiable universal truth or ultimate grounding of value systems, Rorty suggests, the question should not be whose view of the world is "right" or can be best defended by arguments, but which vocabularies one should use in (re)describing the world, or which language games one should play: "[A] talent for speaking differently, rather than for arguing well, is the chief instrument for cultural change";[26] this holds both for politics and for philosophy. The "method" of the latter, according to Rorty, should not be to deduce concepts or to validate theses, but "to redescribe [. . .] things in new ways, until a new 'pattern of linguistic behavior'" is created "which will tempt the rising generation to adopt it, thereby causing them to look for appropriate new forms of nonlinguistic behavior, for example the adoption of new scientific equipment or new social institutions."[27]

To take the contingency and the performative force of language as a starting point—"speaking differently" as a catalyst or even a precondition for "living differently"—is likely to be a gesture familiar to readers of Derrida. What is more, deconstruction, as conceived by Rorty, might be described as the effort to overcome the outdated language games of metaphysics and attendant vocabularies (e.g., "truth," "presence," "being," "being-as-presence," "essence," "identity," "origin," etc.) by redescribing the history of Western thought as a history of repression (of "writing," "absence," "difference," etc.). As we saw in Chapter 2, Derrida's reversal of binary value schemes in Western thought and his displacement of the concepts underpinning them so that they no longer conform to their metaphysical premises involves not just academic, but also political objectives: the goal is to think of democracy in a way unburdened by nationalism and essentialism. One might very well call deconstruction Derrida's attempt to "speak differently" (i.e., to intervene in the language games shaping Western thought) in order to make us *see* things in another light and, eventually, also to *act* differently (i.e., change our social institutions—or at least the ways we understand and manage them).

Indeed, it is possible to discern a close relation between Derrida's and Rorty's political motivations. Derrida's ultimate valorization of the European project of democracy—as "the only system that welcomes in itself, in its very concept, [. . .] the right to self-critique and perfectibility" (cf. above, 4.3)—is not so far removed from Rorty's claim "to retain Enlightenment liberalism while dropping Enlightenment rationalism." Finally, both thinkers emphasize a certain affinity between liberal democracy and literature: Derrida affirms that literature, as a specifically *modern* institution, is closely related to the license to say everything—freedom of speech, that is, not only in artistic terms but as a fundamental right enjoyed by all; Rorty, in turn, counts on literature—rather than philosophy—"to increase our sensitivity to the particular details of the pain and humiliation of other, unfamiliar sorts of people,"[28] and thereby to heighten our sense of justice and loyalty to other human beings.

Yet despite these points of contact, Rorty does not admit that deconstruction holds political implications. Derrida, he claims, is simply a "private ironist," and his work has no public utility and nothing to contribute to the improvement of liberal democracy. This (mis)judgment seems in fact to be based, in the main, on differences of "style" and, indeed, "vocabularies."

Rorty's vision of liberal democracy is founded on a strict division between the public and private spheres—and, accordingly, between public and private vocabularies or language games. Whereas language games in the public sphere are animated by the desire for community, private language games are devoted to self-creation and autonomy. In this setting, "private ironists" are those who recognize the contingency and fragility of their own beliefs, value systems, and "final vocabularies"—which they do not *use* so much as *mention*, as one might say using a standard distinction in analytic philosophy. They tend to put every concept they employ—"deconstruction," "America," "democracy," "justice," and even "themselves"—in quotation marks. Because of their predilection for self-distantiation, ironists also tend to be liberals: aware of the contingency (or historicity) of their own beliefs, they are able to accept that other people have different beliefs and other "final vocabularies" (which are equally contingent, of course).

To qualify Derrida as a "liberal ironist" in this sense—or to qualify his style of writing and talking as "ironic," at least to a certain degree—does not seem altogether mistaken. What is more, Derrida agreed with the assessment. However, he rejected being *reduced* to an ironist, just as he refused to admit that irony, as a quality of speech and writing, should be restricted to private vocabularies.

To address the second point first: Rorty's distinction between public and private has often been criticized for being inconsistent, and even self-contradictory, inasmuch as it is impossible to draw a neat line of separation between "private" and "public" vocabularies. The distinction presupposes that "autonomy" and "solidarity"—the "desire for self-creation" and the "desire for community and justice"—cannot be reconciled (indeed, this is Rorty's critique of classical liberalism). At the same time, however, one can observe that Rorty does not use the distinction between public and private pragmatically; rather, he does so normatively, often differentiating between matters that, in his view, *should* remain private (i.e., be excluded from public discourse) and those that can or should be *allowed* to be public. Irony, then, counts as something that should remain private (even if Rorty also maintains that all liberals should become ironists): the use of irony, after all, entails not only in self-distantiation, but also "threatens" others' final vocabularies—that is, it menaces their sense of community and shared vocabularies.[29] By declaring Derrida a "private ironist" whose work is irrelevant to politics, Rorty seems to be suggesting that one *ought*

to view deconstruction as a private project, as an exercise that can be abandoned where public affairs are concerned. Needless to say, however, it is
not a particularly liberal attitude to exclude another person's language
game from consideration by labeling it simply a private matter.

Derrida insisted on using irony in public, academic contexts, and
for "public" purposes—"with regard to academic tradition, the seriousness
of the philosophical tradition and the personages of the great philosophers."[30] At the same time, he practiced what one might call a "politics of
quotation marks," coining concepts such as "quasi-transcendentality" and
offering paradoxes like "messianism without a messiah." *Contra* Rorty, he
"absolutely refuse[d]" all discourse

that would assign me a single code, a single language game, a single context,
a single situation; and I claim this right not simply out of caprice or because
it is to my taste, but for ethical and political reasons. [. . .] There is evidently
irony in what I do . . . . But, although irony appears to me necessary to what I
do, at the same time [. . .] I take extremely seriously the issue of philosophical
responsibility.[31]

To speak of "quasi-transcendentality," for instance, is "at once ironic and
serious."[32] Such discourse is ironic because the expression was coined in
full awareness of the loss of transcendental positions in modernity, and of
the contingency of supreme values or entities that formerly had been considered meta-historical and universal. It is also serious because it takes into
account "the necessity of posing transcendental questions in order not to
be held within the fragility of an incompetent empiricist discourse, and
thus it is in order to avoid empiricism, positivism and psychologism that
it is endlessly necessary to renew transcendental questioning." At the same
time, of course, such questioning must "be renewed in taking account of
the possibility of fiction, of accidentality and contingency, thereby ensuring that this new form of transcendental questioning only *mimics* the
phantom of classical transcendental seriousness *without renouncing that
which, within this phantom, constitutes an essential heritage.*"[33]

Clearly, it is a *pragmatic* strategy to pose transcendental questions *not*
in order to arrive at transcendental answers but, instead, to avoid "[being]
held within the fragility of an incompetent empiricist discourse" (that is,
with the aim of no longer being at the mercy of accidental impressions
and the vagaries of "commonsensical" language games). At the same time,

however, adherence to the "essential heritage" of this type of questioning is precisely the point where (neo-)pragmatism and deconstruction part ways. We saw in Chapter 3 that this mode of questioning ultimately led Derrida to affirm the existence of "undeconstructible" categories (the gift, the promise, and, above all, justice)—things that cannot be deconstructed. Does this mean that Derrida thinks they escape contingency? Some readers (those lacking a sense of irony, one might say) would certainly claim as much. Others—among whom I number—would prefer to see a certain *normativism* come into play here. Despite—or, more accurately, *precisely because* of—the contingency of language, selfhood, and community, we cannot avoid *positing* certain rules, norms, and even "values" beyond the "short-term reforms and compromises" that define the realm of pragmatic politics according to Rorty. The fact that we must posit norms against the backdrop of contingency (which might be just another word for "undecidability")—the fact that we cannot deduce them from some lost heaven of eternal truths—certainly does not make things easier. For all that, it might still make our norms more liberal: it might change our language games in a way that allows for more justice, and less exclusion.

To sum up, we may put things in Simon Critchley's terms. Is deconstruction pragmatist? Yes, but it is not pragmatist *"all the way down."*

At the basis of deconstruction is a non-pragmatist (or at least non-Rortian) foundational commitment to justice as something that cannot be relativized, or at least cannot be relativized for "we liberals." [. . .] If deconstruction is justice, then this commitment to justice *goes all the way down*: in private self-creation as well as public responsibility.[34]

A question that is even more interesting, however, might be whether pragmatism itself is actually pragmatist *all the way down*. Simon Critchley suggests (and I agree) that the answer is "no"—after all, "its commitment to liberalism—in terms of a non-relativizable claim about the susceptibility of human beings to suffering and the need to minimize cruelty—transgresses the limits of Rorty's pragmatism." Pragmatism cannot "maintain a genuine and non-cynical commitment to liberalism and still remain pragmatist *all the way down*."[35]

Space prohibits discussing what this means for a "programmatology to come." The discussion is ongoing, and I cannot make a substantial contribution within the framework of the book at hand. What deconstruction shows, however, is that contextualism and perspectivism—that is, features it shares with pragmatism and other "postmetaphysical" theories—need not result in post-Nietzschean nihilism or radical empiricism and relativism. "Within the succession of paradigms of knowledge and learning," Anselm Haverkamp has argued,

> deconstruction seems to have succeeded in opening up a new space for transformation within which pragmatism has to be replaced, its mortgage transcribed and its hopes, not to forget them, reiterated. [. . .] It would be an extra task [. . .] to reconsider the reception of deconstruction in America in the light not so much of its detotalizing strategies, but of its pragmatic impact on the rethinking and rereading of crucial concepts. [. . .] I think the once-feared danger of "domesticating" deconstruction's philosophical impact into a domestic brand of pragmatism—certainly a thing to be avoided—is less relevant than the opposite danger of taking the pragmatic acuity out of deconstruction and turning it back into a merely critical, even hypercritical "theory." Deconstruction is a kind of pragmatism, insofar as it is able to replace a disabled pragmatism. It may even turn out to be pragmatism's better equipped, and more pragmatic, version.[36]

The political problems we face today on both sides of the Atlantic—and beyond—are formidable. They challenge both the self-understanding(s) of Western democracies and our sense of justice. America was—and perhaps still is—Europe's attempt to free itself from itself, to get rid of too much history, to make a fresh start in politics instead of wasting energy on tearing down medieval institutions and aristocratic privileges. ("America, you are better off / Than our ancient continent," the famous poem by Johann Wolfgang Goethe reads: "You have no tumbledown castles / And no basalt deposits. / Your inner lives are not disturbed by / Useless memories and vain strife.")

Accordingly, pragmatism may be deemed a "fresh start" for philosophy insofar as it promises to overcome the foundationalist and metaphysical tradition in favor of the free and equal negotiation of what people consider to be "true" and/or "just" for—and in—a given situation. Paradoxically, however, "Europe" today risks becoming nothing but a bureaucratic, all-too-pragmatic endeavor without any political cogency, whereas American politics remain (or once again are) foundationalist and metaphysical. This state of affairs may indicate that new beginnings both in politics and in philosophy are difficult to make without working-through—or deconstructing—what has been handed down from the past. If this does not occur, repressed elements of history may return and change what was supposed to be new into involuntary and unrecognized repetition. In this sense, I would like to conclude by observing that the European tradition—whether in politics or in philosophy—also forms part of the American tradition, and it should be recognized as such.

"A Europe of Hope" is the title of a speech Jacques Derrida delivered at the 50th anniversary celebration of *Le Monde Diplomatique* in May 2004, a few months before he died. (The discourse appeared in the English edition of *Le Monde Diplomatique* under the title "Enlightenment Past and to Come" in November the same year.) Here, Derrida permits himself to dream of a Europe to come:

This Europe, as a proud descendant of the Enlightenment past and a harbinger of the new Enlightenment to come, would show the world what it means to base politics on something more sophisticated than simplistic binary oppositions. In this Europe it would be possible to criticize Israeli policy, especially that pursued by Ariel Sharon and backed by George Bush, without being accused of anti-semitism. In this Europe, supporting the Palestinians in their legitimate struggle for rights, land and a state would not mean supporting suicide bombing or agreeing with the anti-semitic propaganda that is rehabilitating (with sad success) the outrageous lie that is the Protocols of the Elders of Zion. In this Europe it would be usual to worry both about rising anti-semitism and rising Islamophobia.

Ten years later, even though the protagonists of global politics have changed, these words are still relevant. The "Europe of Hope" is still to come (*à venir*). There is no reason, however, why it should not be realized in America.

Appendix: Biography of Jacques Derrida

A more complete biography is found in the appendix to Geoffrey Bennington and Jacques Derrida, *Jacques Derrida* (Chicago: University of Chicago Press, 1999), from which the following chronology is taken.

1930	Birth of Jacques Derrida, the third child of Aimé Derrida and Georgette Safar, on July 15 in El-Biar (Algeria).
1935–41	Kindergarten and elementary school in El-Biar.
1942–47	Lycée de Ben Aknoun, near El-Biar. Derrida is sent home on the first day of school because he is Jewish. Until October 1943, he is not permitted to attend classes.
1947–48	Philosophy class at the Lycée Gauthier in Algiers.
1949–52	Relocation to France. Boarder at the Lycée Louis-le-Grand in Paris.
1952–53	École Normale Supérieure in Paris. Befriends Louis Althusser.
1953–54	Travel to Husserl Archive in Leuven. Writes *Le problème de la genèse dans la philosophie de Husserl*. Befriends Foucault.
1956–57	Passes the *agrégation* and receives a stipend to attend Harvard as a "special auditor." In June 1957, marriage to Marguerite Aucouturier in Boston.
1957–59	Military service in the middle of the Algerian War. A soldier second-class working in a civilian capacity, Derrida teaches French and English to young Algerians and French Algerians. Lives with Marguerite near Algiers, where he works at a private school and translates newspaper articles.
1959–60	First lecture (colloquium at Cerisy), return to France, position as teacher at the *lycée* in Le Mans. First trip to Marguerite's family in Prague.

1960–64   Teaches general philosophy and logic at the Sorbonne (assistant to Gaston Bachelard, Georges Canguilhem, Paul Ricoeur, and Jean Wahl). After Algeria achieves independence, Derrida's family moves to Nice. Teaches at the École Normale Supérieure.

1966   Invited to the "structuralism conference" at Johns Hopkins University, Baltimore, where he meets Paul de Man and Jacques Lacan. Lecture: "Structure, Sign, and Play in the Discourses of the Human Sciences."

1967   Publishes *Voice and Phenomenon, Writing and Difference,* and *Of Grammatology.* Henceforth, an active course of publication, teaching, and lecturing in France and abroad—above all, in the United States.

1968   Moderate participation in the student unrests of May 1968. Invited by Peter Szondi, Derrida offers a series of seminars at the Freie Universität, Berlin.

1970   Derrida's father dies.

1972   Nietzsche colloquium at Cerisy (with Gilles Deleuze, Pierre Klossowski, Sarah Kofman, Philippe Lacoue-Labarthe, Jean-François Lyotard, Jean-Luc Nancy, and others). Publishes *Dissemination* and *Margins of Philosophy.*

1974   Co-founder of the series *La philosophie en effet* at Editions Galilée and of the Group for Research on Teaching Philosophy (GREPH). Publishes *Glas.*

1975   Begins teaching at Yale, with Paul de Man and J. Hillis Miller. The so-called "Yale School," later joined by Harold Bloom and Geoffrey Hartman, sets the tone for the first wave of deconstruction in America. Joint publication: *Deconstruction and Criticism* (New York: Continuum 1979).

1978   Publishes *The Truth in Painting.*

1979   Organizes, with others, the "Estates General of Philosophy" at the Sorbonne.

1980   Derrida defends his *thèse d'etat* at the Sorbonne. At Cerisy, Jean-Luc Nancy and Philippe Lacoue-Labarthe organize the colloquium, "À partir du travail de Jacques Derrida." Publication of *The Post Card: From Socrates to Freud and Beyond.*

1981   Founds, with Jean-Pierre Vernant and others, the Jan Hus Association to assist persecuted Czech intellectuals. On a trip to Prague, Derrida is arrested on charges of drug trafficking and only released upon the energetic intervention of François Mitterand and the French government.

1983   Founding of the *Collège international de philosophie*; Derrida is chosen as the first director. Elected to the École des Hautes Études en Sciences Sociales (research concentration: philosophy and institutions).

1986   Begins teaching at the University of California, Irvine.

1989   Inaugural lecture at the conference, "Deconstruction and the Possibility of Justice," organized at the Cardozo School of Law in New York. The colloquium marks the beginning of the second wave of Derrida-reception in the USA, especially in philosophy and legal theory.

1991   Derrida's mother dies.

1992   Despite vigorous protest from parts of the professorship, Derrida receives an honorary doctorate from Cambridge (U.K.).

1994   Publishes *Politics of Friendship*.

2001   Theodor W. Adorno Prize from the city Frankfurt am Main.

2003   Publishes *Rogues*.

2004   Dies on October 8 in Paris, of cancer.

Notes

PREFACE

1. Jacques Derrida, *Of Grammatology*, trans. Gayatri Chakravorty Spivak (Baltimore: The Johns Hopkins University Press, 1997), 162.

2. Derrida, *Of Grammatology*, 158.

3. Jacques Derrida, *Specters of Marx: The State of Debt, The Work of Mourning, and the New International*, trans. Peggy Kamuf (New York: Routledge, 1994), 18 (emphasis added).

4. Jacques Derrida, *Writing and Difference*, trans. Alan Bass (Chicago: University of Chicago Press, 1980), 371.

5. Jacques Derrida, "Force of Law: The 'Mystical Foundation of Authority,'" *Deconstruction and the Possibility of Justice*, eds. Drucilla Cornell, Michael Rosenfeld, and David Gray Carlson (New York: Routledge, 1992), 8–9.

FIRST APPROACH

1. Jacques Derrida and Geoffrey Bennington, *Jacques Derrida* (Chicago: University of Chicago Press, 1999), 327.

2. Derrida and Bennington, *Jacques Derrida*, 326.

3. This work appeared in France in 1963 under the title, *Edmund Husserl, L'Origine de la géométrie*.

4. On Derrida and Husserl, see Jean-Claude Höflinger, *Jacques Derridas Husserl-Lektüren* (Würzburg: Königshausen & Neumann, 1995), and Uwe Dreisholtkamp, *Jacques Derrida* (Munich: Beck, 1999), especially Chapter 2.

5. Aristotle, *The Metaphysics*, trans. Hugh Lawson-Tancred (New York: Penguin, 1999), 79.

6. Martin Heidegger, *Being and Time*, trans. John Macquarrie and Edward Robinson (New York: Harper & Row, 1962), 44.

7. Cf. Heidegger, *Being and Time*, 149–50.

8. Heidegger, *Being and Time*, 67–8.

9. Heidegger, *Being and Time*, 67.

10. Martin Heidegger, "Letter on Humanism," *Basic Writings*, ed. David Farrell Krell (New York: Harper, 1993), 231.

11. Heidegger, *Being and Time*, 67.

12. Heidegger, *Being and Time*, 68.

13. Cf. Heidegger, *Being and Time*, 73ff.

14. Heidegger, *Being and Time*, 293.

15. Heidegger, *Being and Time*, 279 (translation modified).

16. Cf. Heidegger, *Being and Time*, 293–4.

17. Heidegger, *Being and Time*, 310.

18. Heidegger, *Being and Time*, 394.

19. Heidegger, *Being and Time*, 426–7.

20. Sigmund Freud, *The Ego and the Id*, in *The Complete Psychological Works of Sigmund Freud, Vol. XIX*, trans. James Strachey (London: The Hogarth Press, 1968), 56.

21. Freud, *The Ego and the Id*, 56, 57.

22. Freud, *The Ego and the Id*, 24.

23. Sigmund Freud, "A Difficulty in the Path of Psycho-Analysis," *The Complete Psychological Works of Sigmund Freud, Vol. XVII*, trans. James Strachey (London: The Hogarth Press, 1968), 139–42.

24. As much as he could, Heidegger paid no attention to psychoanalysis, even though, through the intervention of Jean Beaufret in 1955, the philosopher met with Jacques Lacan, first in Freiburg (Germany) and then, a little later, in France. Beaufret also drew Heidegger's attention to Derrida's early publications.

25. Sigmund Freud, *An Autobiographical Study*, in *The Complete Psychological Works of Sigmund Freud, Vol. XX*, trans. James Strachey (London: The Hogarth Press, 1968), 60.

26. Friedrich Nietzsche, *Basic Writings of Nietzsche*, trans. Walter Kaufmann (New York: Modern Library, 2000), 213.

27. Nietzsche, *Basic Writings*, 214.

28. Nietzsche, *Basic Writings*, 456.

29. Nietzsche, *Basic Writings*, 461–2.

30. Jacques Derrida, *Positions*, trans. Alan Bass (Chicago: University of Chicago Press, 1982), 41.

31. Nietzsche, *Basic Writings*, 200.

32. Friedrich Nietzsche, *The Will to Power*, trans. Walter Kaufmann and R.J. Hollingdale (New York: Vintage, 1968), 267.

33. Nietzsche, *The Will to Power*, 283.

34. Jacques Derrida, "Structure, Sign and Play in the Discourse of the Human Sciences," *Writing and Difference*, trans. Alan Bass (Chicago: University of Chicago Press, 1980), 280–1.

35. Hugo von Hofmannsthal, *The Lord Chandos Letter*, trans. Joel Rotenberg (New York: NYRB Classics, 2005), 121.

36. J. L. Ackrill, ed., *A New Aristotle Reader* (Princeton: Princeton University Press, 1989), 12.

37. This account is too simplistic insofar as it not only omits the problem of universals, but also ignores debates concerning doubt, dreaming, and imagination, which have filled libraries since at least the time of Descartes. To be certain he is not dreaming and that his thoughts correspond to anything in the world at all, Descartes, in his *Meditations*, had to reintroduce God as the only way of guaranteeing that language and mental images possessed real points of reference. Until Nietzsche, philosophers were concerned with conquering doubt and stabilizing philosophical systems. That changed in the twentieth century.

38. Ferdinand de Saussure, *Course in General Linguistics*, trans. Wade Baskin (New York: McGraw-Hill, 1959), 112–13.

39. Saussure, *Course in General Linguistics*, 65.

40. Saussure, *Course in General Linguistics*, 65.

41. Saussure, *Course in General Linguistics*, 115 (emphasis added).

42. Saussure, *Course in General Linguistics*, 117, 120 (emphasis added).

43. Saussure, *Course in General Linguistics*, 15.

SECOND APPROACH

1. Derrida in his last interview (*Le Monde*, August 19, 2004).

2. Derrida, "Structure, Sign and Play in the Discourse of the Human Sciences," 280–1.

3. Derrida, *Of Grammatology*, lxxxix.

4. Derrida, *Of Grammatology*, 6.

5. See the preface to "Freud and the Scene of Writing," in *Writing and Difference*.

6. Plato, *Complete Works*, ed. John M. Cooper (Indianapolis: Hackett, 1997), 552.

7. Derrida analyzes this passage extensively in "Plato's Pharmacy," in *Dissemination*, trans. Barbara Johnson (Chicago: University of Chicago Press, 1983), 61–172.

8. Derrida, *Of Grammatology*, 12

9. Saussure, *Course in General Linguistics*, 23.

10. Saussure, *Course in General Linguistics*, 23–4.

11. Jacques Derrida, *Speech and Phenomena, and Other Essays on Husserl's Theory of Signs*, trans. David B. Allison (Evanston: Northwestern University Press, 1973), 82.

12. Derrida, *Speech and Phenomena*, 76.

13. Derrida, *Of Grammatology*, 159.

14. Derrida, *Of Grammatology*, 158.

15. Saussure, *Course in General Linguistics*, 24.

16. Saussure, *Course in General Linguistics*, 25 (translation modified).

17. Saussure, *Course in General Linguistics*, 32.

18. Derrida, *Of Grammatology*, 39–40.

19. Derrida, *Of Grammatology*, 37.

20. Derrida, *Of Grammatology*, 44.

21. Saussure, *Course in General Linguistics*, 119.

22. Saussure, *Course in General Linguistics*, 120.

23. Jean-Jacques Rousseau, quoted in Derrida, *Of Grammatology*, 3.

24. Derrida, *Positions*, 41–2.

25. Jacques Derrida, *Margins of Philosophy*, trans. Alan Bass (Chicago: University of Chicago Press, 1985), 8.

26. Derrida, *Margins of Philosophy*, 8.

27. Derrida, *Margins of Philosophy*, 8.

28. Derrida, *Margins of Philosophy*, 11.

29. Derrida, *Margins of Philosophy*, 9.

30. Derrida, *Margins of Philosophy*, 9.

31. Derrida, *Margins of Philosophy*, 13.

32. Derrida, *Of Grammatology*, 73.

33. Derrida, *Of Grammatology*, 159.

34. Derrida, *Of Grammatology*, 158.

35. Derrida, *Of Grammatology*, 158.

36. Aristotle, *Poetics*, in *Classical Literary Criticism*, ed. Penelope Murray (New York: Penguin, 2000), 85.

37. Derrida, *Margins of Philosophy*, 244–6.

38. Jacques Derrida, *Psyche: Inventions of the Other*, eds. Peggy Kamuf and Elizabeth Rottenberg (Stanford: Stanford University Press, 2007), 50.

39. Derrida, *Dissemination*, 238.

40. Jürgen Habermas, *Postmetaphysical Thinking*, trans. William Mark Hohengarten (Cambridge: The MIT Press, 1994), 207.

41. Derrida, *Margins of Philosophy*, 270.

42. Derrida, *Of Grammatology*, 160.

43. Derrida, *Of Grammatology*, 160.

44. Derrida, *Of Grammatology*, 160.

45. Jean-Jacques Rousseau, *Essay on the Origin of Languages*, quoted in Derrida, *Of Grammatology*, 144.

46. Jean-Jacques Rousseau, *Confessions*, trans. Angela Scholar (Oxford: Oxford University Press, 2000), 114.

47. Derrida, *Of Grammatology*, 142.

48. Jean-Jacques Rousseau, *Emile, or, On Education*, quoted in Derrida, *Of Grammatology*, 146.

49. Rousseau, *Confessions*, 322 (translation slightly modified).

50. Rousseau, *Confessions*, 106 (translation slightly modified).

51. Jean-Jacques Rousseau, *Emile, or, On Education*, trans. Allan Bloom (New York: Basic, 1979), 334.

52. Derrida, *Of Grammatology*, 154–5.

53. Rousseau, *Confessions*, 106.

54. Derrida, *Of Grammatology*, 144.

55. Derrida, *Of Grammatology*, 165.

56. Derrida, *Of Grammatology*, 154.

57. Derrida, *Of Grammatology*, 156.

58. Derrida, *Of Grammatology*, 142.

59. Rousseau, *Confessions*, 5 (translation slightly modified).

60. Max Frisch, *Sketchbook: 1946–1949*, trans. Geoffrey Skelton (New York: Harvest, 1977), 12.

61. Derrida, *Positions*, 11.

62. Jacques Derrida, *Acts of Literature*, ed. Derek Attridge (New York: Routledge, 1991), 37.

63. Derrida, *Positions*, 6.

64. Jacques Derrida, *Writing and Difference*, 278.

65. Derrida, *Writing and Difference*, 279.

THIRD APPROACH

1. Jacques Derrida, "Force of Law: The 'Mystical Foundation of Authority,'" *Deconstruction and the Possibility of Justice*, eds. Drucilla Cornell, Michael Rosenfeld, and David Gray Carlson (New York: Routledge, 1992), 19.

2. Derrida, "Force of Law," 8.

3. Derrida, "Force of Law," 8.

4. Derrida, "Force of Law," 8–9.

5. Derrida, "Force of Law," 6.

6. Michel de Montaigne, *The Complete Essays*, trans. Donald Frame (Stanford: Stanford University Press, 1958), 821.

7. Blaise Pascal, *Pensées and Other Writings,* trans. Honor Levi (Oxford: Oxford University Press, 2008), 24.

8. Derrida, "Force of Law," 14.

9. Derrida, "Force of Law," 14–15.

10. John Rawls, *A Theory of Justice* (Cambridge: Harvard University Press, 2005), 4.

11. Rawls, *A Theory of Justice*, 7.

12. Derrida, "Force of Law," 16.

13. Jacques Derrida, *Writing and Difference*, 111.

14. Derrida, "Force of Law," 22.

15. Derrida, "Force of Law," 22.

16. Jacques Derrida, "Marx & Sons," *Ghostly Demarcations: A Symposium on Jacques Derrida's Specters of Marx*, ed. Michael Sprinker (New York: Verso, 2008), 267.

17. Friedrich Nietzsche, "On Truth and Lie in an Extra-Moral Sense," from the *"Nachlass"* (1873).

18. Derrida, "Force of Law," 23.

19. Derrida, "Force of Law," 23.

20. Derrida, "Force of Law," 24.

21. Derrida, "Force of Law," 27.

22. Jacques Derrida, *Specters of Marx: The State of Debt, The Work of Mourning, and the New International*, trans. Peggy Kamuf (New York: Routledge, 1994), 59.

23. Derrida, "Force of Law," 25.

24. Derrida, *Specters of Marx*, 168.

25. Derrida, "Force of Law," 29.

26. Derrida, "Force of Law," 31.

27. Derrida, "Force of Law," 31.

28. Derrida, "Force of Law," 31.

29. Derrida, "Force of Law," 31.

30. Derrida, "Force of Law," 51.

31. Derrida, "Force of Law," 29.

32. Derrida, "Force of Law," 66.

33. Derrida, "Force of Law," 62–3.

34. Derrida, "Force of Law," 25.

35. Jacques Derrida, *Given Time: I. Counterfeit Money*, trans. Peggy Kamuf (Chicago: University of Chicago Press, 1994), 12.

36. Jacques Derrida, *Given Time: I. Counterfeit Money*, 30.

37. Martin Heidegger, *On the Way to Language* (New York: HarperOne, 1982), 87–8.

38. Derrida, *Given Time: I. Counterfeit Money*, 24 (emphasis added).

39. Derrida, "Force of Law," 15; cf. supra.

40. Cf. supra.

41. Derrida, *Margins of Philosophy*, 321.

42. Derrida, *Margins of Philosophy*, 322.

43. Jacques Derrida, "Remarks on Deconstruction and Pragmatism," *Deconstruction and Pragmatism*, ed. Chantal Mouffe (New York: Routledge, 1996), 84.

44. Derrida, "Force of Law," 11.

FOURTH APPROACH

1. Derrida, "Structure, Sign and Play in the Discourse of the Human Sciences," 280–1; cf. supra.

2. Heidegger, *Being and Time*, 293; cf. supra.

3. Jacques Derrida and Bernard Stiegler, *Echographies of Television: Filmed Interviews*, trans. Jennifer Bajorek (Oxford: Polity, 2002), 112.

4. Derrida, *Specters of Marx*, 56.

5. Derrida, *Specters of Marx*, 37.

6. Karl Marx, *The Eighteenth Brumaire of Louis Bonaparte*, trans. Daniel de Leon (Chicago: Charles H. Kerr & Company, 1913), 10–13.

7. Derrida, *Specters of Marx*, 16 (translation modified).

8. Derrida, *Specters of Marx*, 54.

9. Derrida, *Specters of Marx*, xix.

10. Quoted in Jacques Derrida, *Politics of Friendship*, trans. George Collins (New York: Verso, 1997), 227.

11. Derrida, *Politics of Friendship*, viii.

12. Derrida, *Politics of Friendship*, 262.

13. Derrida, *Politics of Friendship*, 159.

14. Derrida, *Politics of Friendship*, viii.

15. Derrida, *Politics of Friendship*, 132.

16. Derrida, *Politics of Friendship*, 158–9 (translation modified).

17. Derrida, *Of Grammatology*, 24.

18. Derrida, *Politics of Friendship*, 159.

19. Jacques Derrida, *Rogues: Two Essays on Reason*, trans. Pascale-Anne Brault and Michael Naas (Stanford: Stanford University Press, 2005), 37.

20. Derrida, *Rogues*, 63 (translation modified).

21. Derrida, *Rogues*, 86.

22. Derrida, *Politics of Friendship*, 105 (translation modified).

23. Derrida, *Politics of Friendship*, 159.

24. Derrida, *Rogues*, 39.

25. Derrida, *Speech and Phenomena*, 82.

26. Jacques Derrida, *The Other Heading: Reflections on Today's Europe* (Bloomington: Indiana University Press, 1992), 9–11.

27. Jacques Derrida, *Über den Namen. Drei Essays*, trans. Hans-Dieter Gondek and Markus Sedlaczek (Vienna: Passagen, 2000), 146.

28. Plato, *Timaeus*, trans. Peter Kalkavage (Newburyport: Focus, 2001), 84.

29. Plato, *Timaeus*, 82 (translation slightly modified).

30. Jacques Derrida, *Wie nicht Sprechen. Verneinungen*, trans. Hans-Dieter Gondek (Vienna: Passagen, 2006), 68.

31. Derrida, *Wie nicht Sprechen,* 70.

32. Derrida, *Rogues,* 80.

33. Derrida, *Rogues,* 82.

34. Derrida, *Specters of Marx,* 85.

35. Derrida, *Rogues,* 87.

36. Jacques Derrida, *Negotiations: Interventions and Interviews, 1971–2001,* ed. Elizabeth Rottenberg (Stanford: Stanford University Press, 2003), 374.

37. Derrida, *Politics of Friendship,* 104.

38. Derrida, *Rogues,* 85–6 (emphasis added).

39. Jacques Derrida and Gianni Vattimo, *Religion,* trans. David Webb (Stanford: Stanford University Press, 1998), 73.

40. Derrida, *Rogues,* 10–11.

41. Derrida, *Rogues,* 14.

42. Derrida, *Rogues,* 14–15.

43. Derrida, *Rogues,* 1.

44. Derrida, *Politics of Friendship,* 106 (translation modified).

45. Derrida, *Politics of Friendship,* 106.

46. Derrida, *Specters of Marx,* 82.

47. Derrida, *Specters of Marx,* 82–3.

48. Derrida, *Specters of Marx,* 83.

49. Jacques Derrida and Elisabeth Roudinesco, *For What Tomorrow . . . : A Dialogue* (Stanford: Stanford University Press, 2004), 178.

50. Jacques Derrida, *The Other Heading: Reflections on Today's Europe* (Bloomington: Indiana University Press, 1992), 78.

51. Giovanna Borradori, *Philosophy in a Time of Terror: Dialogues with Jürgen Habermas and Jacques Derrida* (Chicago: University of Chicago Press, 2004), 115.

52. Borradori, *Philosophy in a Time of Terror,* 116.

53. Borradori, *Philosophy in a Time of Terror,* 117.

54. Borradori, *Philosophy in a Time of Terror,* 118.

55. Borradori, *Philosophy in a Time of Terror,* 95.

56. Borradori, *Philosophy in a Time of Terror,* 115.

57. Borradori, *Philosophy in a Time of Terror,* 106.

EPILOGUE

1. Jacques Derrida, *Memoires for Paul de Man* (New York: Columbia Press, 1989), 17–18.

2. Jacques Derrida, "The Time is Out of Joint," *Deconstruction is/in America. A New Sense of the Political,* ed. Anselm Haverkamp (New York: New York University Press, 1995), 31–2.

3. Derrida, *Memoires for Paul de Man,* 15.

4. J. Hillis Miller, "The Disputed Ground: Deconstruction and Literary Studies," *Deconstruction is/in America. A New Sense of the Political*, ed. Anselm Haverkamp (New York: New York University Press, 1995), 80.

5. Derrida, *Of Grammatology*, 158.

6. Terry Eagleton, *Literary Theory: An Introduction* (Minneapolis: University of Minnesota Press, 2008), 40.

7. Jonathan Culler, "Criticism and Institutions: The American University," *Poststructuralism and the Question of History*, ed. Derek Attridge et. al. (Cambridge: Cambridge University Press, 1987), 87.

8. Documented in Jacques Derrida, *Limited Inc.* (Chicago: Northwestern University Press, 1988).

9. John R. Searle, "Reiterating the Differences. A Reply to Derrida," *Glyph* 2 (1977): 198.

10. Searle, "Reiterating the Differences," 203.

11. Searle, "Reiterating the Differences," 198.

12. Judith Butler, *Excitable Speech. A Politics of the Performative* (New York: Routledge, 1997), 2.

13. Butler, *Excitable Speech*, 41.

14. Homi Bhabha, *The Location of Culture* (New York: Routledge, 1994), 2.

15. Peter Goodrich, Florian Hoffmann, Michel Rosenfeld, and Cornelia Vismann, "Introduction: A Philosophy of Legal Enigmas," *Derrida and Legal Philosophy* (New York: Palgrave Macmillan, 2008), 2–3.

16. Friedrich Nietzsche, *The Antichrist*, § 52.

17. Peter Goodrich, "Europe in America: Grammatology, Legal Studies, and the Politics of Transmission," *Columbia Law Review* 101.8 (2001): 2033–2084; here, 2034.

18. Goodrich, "Europe in America," 2040.

19. Goodrich, "Europe in America," 2040.

20. Nietzsche, *The Antichrist*, § 52.

21. Goodrich, "Europe in America," 2069.

22. Goodrich, "Europe in America," 2070.

23. Goodrich, "Europe in America," 2039.

24. Jacques Derrida, "Toward an Ethic of Discussion," in *Limited Inc.*, 148.

25. Derrida, "Toward an Ethic of Discussion," 148.

26. Richard Rorty, *Contingency, Irony, and Solidarity* (Cambridge: Cambridge University Press 1989), 7.

27. Rorty, *Contingency*, 9.

28. Rorty, *Contingency*, xvi.

29. Cf. Rorty, *Contingency*, 89–90.

30. Derrida, "Remarks on Deconstruction and Pragmatism," 81.

31. Derrida, "Remarks on Deconstruction and Pragmatism," 81.

32. Derrida, "Remarks on Deconstruction and Pragmatism," 81.

33. Derrida, "Remarks on Deconstruction and Pragmatism," 81–2 (emphasis added).

34. Simon Critchley, "Deconstruction and Pragmatism—Is Derrida a Private Ironist or a Public Liberal?" in *Deconstruction and Pragmatism*, 37.

35. Critchley, "Deconstruction and Pragmatism," 37.

36. Anselm Haverkamp, "Deconstruction is/as Neopragmatism," *Deconstruction is/in America* (New York: New York University Press, 1995), 6–7.

Selected Bibliography

A complete bibliography of Derrida's writings (including interviews and translations in other languages) in alphabetical and chronological order, a selected bibliography of secondary literature, as well as other materials are found on the website "Derrida Online" on the homepage of the University of Irvine, CA, maintained by Peter Krapp (url: http://hydra.humanities.uci.edu/derrida/).

The Critical Theory Archive of the University of Irvine also contains Derrida's unpublished legacy (url: http://hydra.humanities.uci.edu/derrida/uci.html).

The following selected bibliography lists independent monographs and important articles as well as their English editions in chronological order.

1. Works by Jacques Derrida

1962

Edmund Husserl, *L'Origine de la géométrie. Traduction et introduction par Jacques Derrida*. Paris: PUF.

1964

"Violence et métaphysique: Essai sur la pensée d'Emmanuel Levinas (première partie)." *Revue de Métaphysique et de Morale* 3: 322–54.
"Violence et métaphysique: Essai sur la pensée d'Emmanuel Levinas (deuxième partie)." *Revue de Métaphysique et de Morale* 4: 425–73.

1967

De la Grammatologie. Paris: Minuit.
L'écriture et la différence. Paris: Seuil.

La Voix et le phénomène: Introduction au problème du signe dans la phénoménologie de Husserl. Paris: PUF.

1971

"La mythologie blanche." *Poetique* 5: 1–52.

1972

La Dissémination. Paris: Seuil.
Marges de la philosophie. Paris: Minuit.
Positions: Entretiens avec Henri Ronse, Julia Kristeva, Jean-Louis Houdebine, Guy Scarpetta. Paris: Minuit.

1973

Speech and Phenomena, and Other Essays on Husserl's Theory of Signs. Trans. David B. Allison. Evanston: Northwestern University Press.

1974

Glas. Paris: Galilée.
"White Mythology. Metaphor in the Text of Philosophy." *New Literary History* 6: 5–74.

1975

"Economimesis." In *Mimesis des articulations,* ed. Sylviane Agacinski. Paris: Aubier-Flammarion.

1976

Eperons: Les styles de Nietzsche / Spurs: Nietzsche's Styles / Sporen: die Stile Nietzsches / Sproni: gli stili di Nietzsche. Venice: Corbo e Fiori.
"Fors. Préface." In Nicolas Abraham, Maria Torok, *Cryptonymie: Le verbier de l'Homme aux loups.* Paris: Flammarion.
"Fors: The Anglish Words of Nicolas Abraham and Maria Torok." *Georgia Review* 31.1: 64–116.
Of Grammatology. Trans. Gayatri Chakravorty Spivak. Baltimore: Johns Hopkins University Press.

1978

La Vérité en peinture. Paris: Flammarion.
"The Retrait of Metaphor." *Enclitic* 2.2: 5–34.
Writing and Difference. Trans. Alan Bass. Chicago: University of Chicago Press.

1979

"Parergon." *October* 9: 3–40.

1980

La Carte postale. De Socrate à Freud et au-delà. Paris: Flammarion.

1981

Dissemination. Trans. Barbara Johnson. Chicago: University of Chicago Press.
"Economimesis." *Diacritics* 11: 3–25.
Positions. Trans. Alan Bass. Chicago: University of Chicago Press.
"Title (to be specified)." *Sub-Stance* 31: 5–22.

1982

Margins of Philosophy. Trans. Alan Bass. Chicago: University of Chicago Press.

1983

*D'un ton apocalyptique adopté naguère en philosophie. Pas d'apocalypse, pas mainte-
nant (à toute vitesse, sept missiles, sept missives).* Paris: Galilée.
"Geschlecht: Sexual Difference, Ontological Difference." *Research in Phenomenology* 13: 65–83.

1984

Otobiographies: L'enseignement de Nietzsche et la politique du nom propre. Paris:
Galilée.
"No Apocalypse, Not Now (Full Speed Ahead, Seven Missiles, Seven Missives)."
Trans. Catherine Porter and Philip Lewis. *Diacritics* 14.2: 20–31.
"Of an Apocalyptic Tone Recently Adopted in Philosophy." *Oxford Literary
Review* 6.2: 3–37.

1985

"In Memoriam: For Paul de Man." *Yale French Studies*: 323–6.
"Préjugés: devant la loi." In *La faculté de juger. Colloque de Cerisy.* Paris: Minuit.
Droit de regards: photographie (with Marie-Françoise Plissart). Paris: Minuit.

1986

Schibboleth - pour Paul Celan. Paris: Galilée.
Parages. Paris: Galilée.
Glas. Trans. John P. Leavy Jr. and Richard Rand. Lincoln: University of Nebraska
Press.

Mémoires: For Paul de Man. Trans. Cecile Lindsay, Jonathan Culler, and Eduardo Cadava. New York: Columbia University Press.

1987

De l'esprit: Heidegger et la question. Paris: Galilée.
Feu la cendre. Paris: Éditions des Femmes.
"Geschlecht II: Heidegger's Hand." Trans. John P. Leavy Jr. In *Deconstruction and Philosophy,* ed. John Sallis. Chicago: University of Chicago Press.
Psyché: Inventions de l'autre. Paris: Galilée.
Ulysse gramophone. Deux mots pour Joyce. Paris: Galilée.
Cinders. Trans. Ned Lukacher. Lincoln: University of Nebraska Press.
The Post Card: From Socrates to Freud and Beyond. Trans. Alan Bass. Chicago: University of Chicago Press.
The Truth in Painting. Trans. Geoffrey Bennington and Ian McLeod. Chicago: University of Chicago Press.

1988

Limited Inc. Trans. Samuel Weber and Jeffrey Mehlman. Evanston: Northwestern University Press.
Mémoires: Pour Paul de Man. Paris: Galilée.
Comme le bruit de la mer au fond d'un coquillage. La guerre de Paul de Man. Mémoires II. Paris: Galilée.
"Like the Sound of the Sea Deep Within a Shell: Paul de Man's War." Trans. Peggy Kamuf. *Critical Inquiry* 14: 590–652. (Reprinted in *Responses. On Paul de Man's Wartime Journalism,* ed. Werner Hamacher, Neil H. Hertz, and Thomas Keenan. Lincoln: University of Nebraska Press.)

1989

"Some Statements and Truisms about Neologisms, Newisms, Postisms, Parasitisms, and other small Seismisms." In *The States of Theory,* ed. D. Carroll. New York: Columbia University Press.
"How to Avoid Speaking: Denials." In *Derrida and Negative Theology,* eds. Harold Coward and Toby Foshay. Albany: SUNY Press.
Of Spirit. Heidegger and the Question. Trans. Geofffrey Bennington and Rachel Bowlby. Chicago: University of Chicago Press.
Edmund Husserl's Origin of Geometry: An Introduction. Trans. John P. Leavy Jr. Lincoln: University of Nebraska Press.

1990

Du droit à la philosophie. Paris: Galilée.

"Force of Law: The Mystical Foundation of Authority." *Cardozo Law Review* 11.5–6: 920–1045.
Heidegger et la question. De l'esprit et autres essais. Paris: Flammarion.
"Interpretations at War. Kant, le Juif, l'Allemand." In *Phénoménologie et Politique. Mélanges offertes à Jacques Taminiaux.* Brussels: Ousia.
Limited Inc. Paris: Galilée.
Mémoires d'aveugle. L'autoportrait et autres ruines. Paris: Réunion des musées nationaux.
Le problème de la genèse dans la philosophie de Husserl. Paris: PUF.

1991

L'autre cap, suivi de la democratie ajournée. Paris: Minuit.
Donner le temps I: La fausse monnaie. Paris: Galilée.
Jacques Derrida (with Geoffrey Bennington). Paris: Seuil.
"Pour l'amour de Lacan." In *Lacan avec les philosophes*, ed. Natalia Avtonomova. Paris: Albin Michel.
"Interpretations at War: Kant, the Jew, the German." *New Literary History* 22: 39–95.

1992

Acts of Literature. Ed. Derek Attridge. London: Routledge.
Given Time I: Counterfeit Money. Trans. Peggy Kamuf. Chicago: University of Chicago Press.
"Schibboleth." In *Word Traces: Readings of Paul Celan*, ed. Aris Fioretos. Baltimore: John Hopkins University Press.
The Other Heading: Reflections on Today's Europe. Trans. Pascale-Anne Brault and Michael Naas. Bloomington: Indiana University Press.

1993

Geschlecht IV: Heidegger's Ear. Philopolemology. Commemorations, ed. John Sallis. Bloomington: Indiana University Press.
Passions. Paris: Galilée.
Khôra. Paris: Galilée.
Sauf le nom. Paris: Galilée.
Spectres de Marx. Paris: Galilée.
Aporias: Dying—Awaiting (One Another at) the "Limits of Truth." Trans. Thomas Dutoit. Stanford: Stanford University Press.
Jacques Derrida (with Geoffrey Bennington). Chicago: University of Chicago Press.
Memoirs of the Blind: The Self-Portrait and Other Ruins. Trans. Pascale-Anne Brault and Michael Naas. Chicago: University of Chicago Press.

1994

Politiques de l'amitié. Paris: Galilée.
Force de loi. Le fondement mystique de l'autorité. Paris: Galilée.
Specters of Marx: The State of the Debt, the Work of Mourning & the New International. Trans. Peggy Kamuf. London: Routledge.

1995

Mal d'archive. Une impression freudienne. Paris: Galilée.
Moscou aller-retour. Paris: Éditions de l'Aube.
On the Name. Trans. David Wood, John P. Leavy Jr., and Ian McLeod. Stanford: Stanford University Press.
The Gift of Death. Trans. Davis Wills. Chicago: University of Chicago Press.

1996

Apories. Mourir—s'attendre "aux limites de la vérité." Paris: Galilée.
Monolinguisme de l'autre ou la prothèse d'origine. Paris: Galilée.
Résistances à la psychanalyse. Paris: Galilée.
Archive Fever: A Freudian Impression. Trans. Eric Prenowitz. Chicago: University of Chicago Press.

1997

Cosmopolites de tous les pays, encore un effort! Paris: Galilée.
De l'hospitalité. Paris: Calmann-Lévy.
Du droit à la philosophie du point de vue cosmopolitique. Paris: Verdier.
Politics of Friendship. Trans. George Collins. London: Verso.

1998

Psyché, Inventions de l'autre I. Paris: Galilée.
Demeure. Maurice Blanchot. Paris: Galilée.
Monolingualism of the Other or The Prosthesis of Origin. Trans. Patrick Mensah. Stanford: Stanford University Press.
Resistances of Psychoanalysis. Trans. Pascale-Anne Brault and Michael Naas. Stanford: Stanford University Press.
Right of Inspection (with Marie Francoise Plissart). Trans. David Wills. New York: Manacelli Press.

1999.

Donner la mort. Paris: Galilée.
"Marx and Sons." In *Ghostly Demarcations,* ed. Michael Sprinker. London: Verso.

2000

Etats d'âme de la psychanalyse. Adresse aux Etats Généraux de la Psychanalyse. Paris: Galilée.
Le toucher, Jean-Luc Nancy. Paris: Galilée.
H.C. pour la vie, c'est a dire . . . Hélène Cixous, croisées d'une oeuvre. Paris: Galilée.
Demeure: Fiction and Testimony. Trans. Elizabeth Rottenberg. Stanford: Stanford University Press.
Of Hospitality. Trans. Rachel Bowlby. Stanford: Stanford University Press.

2001

Papier Machine. Paris: Gallimard.
L'université sans condition. Paris: Galilée.
On Cosmopolitanism and Forgiveness. Trans. Mark Dooley and Michael Hughes. London: Routledge.
The Work of Mourning. Trans. Pascale-Anne Brault and Michael Naas. Stanford: Stanford University Press.
Veils (with Hélène Cixous). Trans. Geoffrey Bennington. Stanford: Stanford University Press.

2002

Fichus. Discours de Francfort. Paris: Galilée
Marx & Sons. Paris: PUF/Galilée.
Ethics, Institutions and the Right to Philosophy. Trans. Peter Pericles Trifonas. Lanham: Rowman Littlefield.
Who's Afraid of Philosophy? Right to Philosophy I. Stanford: Stanford University Press.
Without Alibi. Trans. Peggy Kamuf. Stanford: Stanford University Press.

2003

Voyous: Deux essais sur la raison. Paris: Seuil.
Chaque fois unique, la fin du monde. Paris: Galilée.
Psyché, Inventions de l'autre II. Paris: Galilée.
Philosophy in a Time of Terror: Dialogues With Jürgen Habermas and Jacques Derrida, by Giovanna Borradori. Chicago: University of Chicago Press.
The Problem of Genesis in Husserl's Philosophy. Trans. Martin Hobson. Chicago: University of Chicago Press.

2004

Pourquoi la guerre? Paris: Galilée.

Eyes of the University: Right to Philosophy II. Trans. Jan Plug et al. Stanford : Stanford University Press.

2005

On Touching, Jean-Luc Nancy. Trans. Christine Irizarry. Stanford: Stanford University Press.

Rogues: Two Essays on Reason. Trans. Pascale-Anne Brault and Michael Naas. Stanford: Stanford University Press.

2006

H.C. for Life, That is to Say. Trans. Laurent Milesi and Stefan Herbrechter. Stanford: Stanford University Press.

Paper Machine. Trans. Rachel Bowlby. Stanford: Stanford University Press.

2007

"A Certain Impossible Possibility of Saying the Truth." In *The Late Derrida*, ed. J. T. Mitchell and Arnold I. Davidson. Chicago: University of Chicago Press.

Psyche: Inventions of the Other. Volume I. Trans. Peggy Kamuf and Elizabeth Rottenberg. Stanford: Stanford University Press.

2008

Séminaire. La bête et le souverain. Volume I (2001–2002). Paris: Galilée.

Psyche: Inventions of the Other. Volume II. Trans. Peggy Kamuf and Elizabeth Rottenberg. Stanford: Stanford University Press.

The Animal That Therefore I Am. Ed. Marie-Louise Mallet. Trans. David Wills. New York: Fordham University Press.

2009

Demeure, Athènes. Photographies de Jean-Francois Bonhomme. Paris: Galilée.

The Beast and the Sovereign, Volume I. Trans. Geoffrey Bennington. Chicago: University of Chicago Press.

2010

Séminaire. La bête et le souverain. Volume II (2002–2003). Paris: Galilée.

Athens, Still Remains: The Photographs of Jean-Francois Bonhomme. Trans. Pascale-Anne Brault and Michael Naas. New York: Fordham University Press.

Copy, Archive, Signature. A Conversation on Photography. Trans. Jeff Fort. Stanford: Stanford University Press.

Parages. Trans. Tom Conley, James Hulbert, John P. Leavy Jr., and Avital Ronell. Stanford: Stanford University Press.

2011

Politique et amitié. Entretien avec Michael Sprinker autour de Marx et d'Althusser. Paris: Galilée.
The Beast and the Sovereign. Volume II. Trans. Geoffrey Bennington. Chicago: University of Chicago Press.
Voice and Phenomenon: Introduction to the Problem of the Sign in Husserl's Phenomenology. Trans. Leonard Lawlor. Evanston: Northwestern University Press.

2012

Les Yeux de la langue. L'abîme et le volcan. Paris: Galilée.
Histoire du mensonge. Prolégomènes. Paris: Galilée.
Pardonner. L'impardonnable et l'imprescriptible. Paris: Galilée.
Séminaire. La peine de mort. Volume I (1999–2000). Paris: Galilée.

2013

À dessein, le dessin. Le Havre: Franciscopolis.
Signature Derrida. Ed. Jay Williams. Chicago: University of Chicago Press.

2. Selected Books and Articles on Derrida

BIOGRAPHY

Peeters, Benoît. *Derrrida. A Biography.* Trans. Andrew Brown. Cambridge, UK: Polity Press, 2012.

OTHER INTRODUCTIONS

Antonioli, Manola, ed. *Abécédaire de Jacques Derrida.* Paris: Vrin, 2006.
Bennington, Geoffrey and Jacques Derrida. *Jacques Derrida.* Chicago: University of Chicago Press, 1993.
Collins, Jeff and Bill Mayblin. *Introducing Derrida.* Cambridge, UK: Icon Books, 2005.
Deutscher, Penelope. *How to Read Derrida.* New York: Norton, 2006.
Gaston, Sean. *Starting With Derrida.* London: Continuum, 2008.
Glendinning, Simon. *Derrida: A Very Short Introduction.* Oxford: Oxford University Press, 2011.
Hill, Leslie. *The Cambridge Introduction to Jacques Derrida.* Cambridge: Cambridge University Press, 2007.
Howells, Christina. *Derrida. Deconstruction from Phenomenology to Ethics.* Cambridge, UK: Polity Press, 1998.

Norris, Christopher. *Derrida*. Cambridge: Harvard University Press, 1988.

Royle, Nicholas. *Jacques Derrida*. London: Routledge, 2003.

Thomas, Michael. *The Reception of Derrida: Translation and Transformation*. New York: Palgrave Macmillan, 2006

OTHER

Anderson, Nicole. *Derrida: Ethics under Erasure*. London: Continuum, 2012.

Arac, Jonathan, Wlad Godzich, and Wallace Martin. *The Yale Critics. Deconstruction in America*. Minneapolis: University of Minnesota Press, 1983.

Attridge, Derek, Geoffrey Bennington, and Robert Young, eds. *Poststructuralism and the Question of History*. Cambridge: Cambridge University Press, 1987.

Bennington, Geoffrey. *Legislations. The Politics of Deconstruction*. London: Verso, 1994.

———. *Interrupting Derrida*. London: Routledge, 2000.

Bloom, Harold, Paul de Man, Jacques Derrida, Geoffrey Hartman, and J. Hillis Miller. *Deconstruction and Criticism*. London: Continuum, 1979.

Caputo, John D. *The Prayers and Tears of Jacques Derrida: Religion Without Religion*. Bloomington: Indiana University Press, 1997.

———. *Deconstruction in a Nutshell*. New York: Fordham University Press, 1997.

Cheah, Pheng and Suzanne Guerlac, eds. *Derrida and the Time of the Political*. Durham: Duke University Press, 2009.

Cohen, Tom, ed. *Jacques Derrida and the Humanities: A Critical Reader*. Cambridge: Cambridge University Press, 2001.

Cornell, Drucilla, ed. *Deconstruction and the Possibility of Justice*. New York: Routledge, 1992.

Culler, Jonathan. *On Deconstruction. Theory and Criticism after Structuralism*. Ithaca: Cornell University Press, 1982.

———. *The Pursuit of Signs: Semiotics, Literature, Deconstruction*. Ithaca: Cornell University Press, 1981.

De Man, Paul. "The Rhetoric of Blindness: Jacques Derrida's Reading of Rousseau." *Blindness and Insight: Essays in the Rhetoric of Contemporary Criticism*. Minneapolis: University of Minnesota Press, 1983.

Dick, Maria-Daniella and Julian Wolfreys. *The Derrida Wordbook*. Edinburgh: Edinburgh University Press, 2013.

Gasché, Rodolphe. *The Tain of the Mirror: Derrida and the Philosophy of Reflection*. Cambridge: Harvard University Press, 1986.

———. *Inventions of Difference: On Jacques Derrida*. Cambridge: Harvard University Press, 1994.

Gaston, Sean and Ian Maclachlan, eds. *Reading Derrida's "Of Grammatology."* New York: Continuum, 2011.

German Law Journal 6.1 (2005). *Special Issue: A Special Dedication to Jacques Derrida.*

Goodrich, Peter, Florian Hoffmann, Michel Rosenfeld, and Cornelia Vismann, eds. *Derrida and Legal Philosophy.* New York: Palgrave Macmillan, 2008.

Goodrich, Peter. "Europe in America: Grammatology, Legal Studies, and the Politics of Transmission." *Columbia Law Review* 101.8 (2001): 2033–84.

Hägglund, Martin. *Radical Atheism. Derrida and the Time of Life.* Stanford: Stanford University Press, 2008.

Haverkamp, Anselm, ed. *Deconstruction is/in America. A New Sense of the Political.* New York: New York University Press, 1995.

Kamuf, Peggy. *A Derrida Reader. Between the Blinds.* New York: Columbia University Press, 1991.

———. *To Follow: The Wake of Jacques Derrida.* Edinburgh: Edinburgh University Press, 2010.

Lawlor, Leonard. *Derrida and Husserl: The Basic Problem of Phenomenology.* Bloomington: Indiana University Press, 2002.

Leonard, Miriam, ed. *Derrida and Antiquity.* Oxford: Oxford University Press, 2010.

Macksey, Richard and Eugenio Donato, eds. *The Structuralist Controversy: The Languages of Criticism and the Sciences of Man.* Baltimore: Johns Hopkins University Press, 2007.

Mouffe, Chantal, ed. *Deconstruction and Pragmatism.* London: Routledge, 1996.

Naas, Michael. *Derrida From Now On.* New York: Fordham University Press, 2008.

Norris, Christopher and David Roden, eds. *Jacques Derrida.* 4 volumes. London: Sage, 2003.

Spitzer, Anais N. *Derrida, Myth and the Impossibility of Philosophy.* New York: Continuum, 2011.

Weber, Elisabeth, ed. *Living Together. Jacques Derrida's Communities of Violence and Peace.* New York: Fordham University Press, 2012.

Weiner, Allison and Simon Morgan Wortham, eds. *Encountering Derrida. Legacies and Futures of Deconstruction.* New York: Continuum, 2007.